Exploring Rural
PORTUGAL

OTHER BOOKS IN THE *EXPLORING RURAL* SERIES

Series Editor: Andrew Sanger

Austria: Gretel Beer
England & Wales: Christopher Pick
France: Andrew Sanger
Germany: John Ardagh
Greece: Pamela Westland
Ireland: Andrew Sanger
Italy: Michael Leech
Scotland: Gilbert Summers
Spain: Jan S. McGirk

Exploring Rural
PORTUGAL

JOE STAINES AND
LIA DUARTE

PASSPORT BOOKS
a division of *NTC Publishing Group*
Lincolnwood, Illinois USA

This edition first published in 1992 by Passport Books,
a division of NTC Publishing Group, 4255
West Touhy Avenue, Lincolnwood (Chicago), Illinois
60646-1975 U.S.A. Originally published by Christopher
Helm (Publishers) Ltd, a subsidiary of A & C Black
(Publishers) Ltd. Copyright © Joe Staines and Lia Duarte.
Maps and line illustrations by David Henderson.

Printed in Great Britain

CONTENTS

Contents

ACKNOWLEDGEMENTS

Several people have given help and encouragement in the writing of this book, but particular thanks go to the Oxford School of Languages in Lisbon and, above all, to Prunella Staines for her typing skills and for her patience.

Portugal—The Regions and the Routes

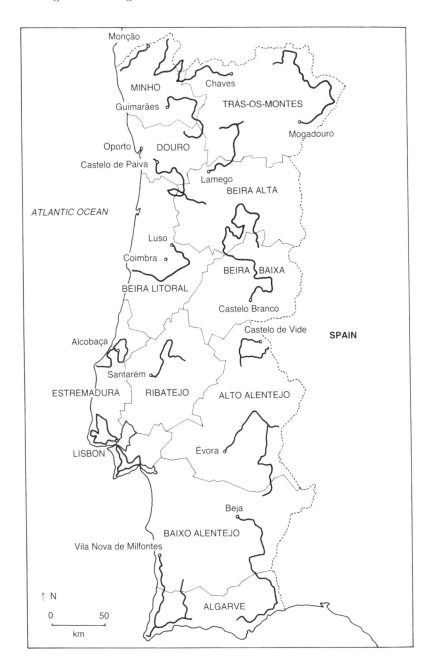

INTRODUCTION

Each night on Portuguese television, when the time comes for the main channel to close down, the national anthem is played. Not, as in the UK, over shots of the Royal family (theirs went into exile when Portugal became a republic in 1910) but over long, breathtaking, aerial views of the country's coastline with the full weight of the Atlantic Ocean being thrown against it.

This represents one of the strongest elements of Portuguese national pride: Portugal, the westernmost country of the European mainland which, by a combination of shrewdness and great bravery, managed to conquer the might of the oceans to become the first great sea-going commercial empire. Its days as a world power were short-lived, however, over as early as 1578, when the King, Dom Sebastião I, lost both his life and an entire army of 15,000 fighting against the 'infidel' in Morocco.

Today maritime traditions live on in the old-fashioned boats and methods of fishing still found in many parts of Portugal; a pleasantly picturesque sight for the tourist but a problem for a major industry

Cabo da Roca—the westernmost point of Europe

1

attempting to survive in a competitive world. More recently the 800km of coastline, with its seemingly endless sandy beaches, has begun to be appreciated by other people as well as the Portuguese. In the case of the Algarve coast, this has brought with it the very dubious blessing of mass tourism.

On the whole, the coast is not a priority in this book. We have preferred to push inland and explore the other Portugal: the vast, sun-scorched plains of the Alentejo; the great northern rivers with their green and fertile valleys; the medieval castles along the border with Spain. This is a country of much greater variety than is usually supposed and regional differences of languages, building and farming are all visible as you drive through the countryside. Large cities are avoided, with the exception of Lisbon, although each route includes at least one important historical monument or site.

In the more isolated areas, particularly the north east, where villages and village life have changed little over the centuries, the arrival of a stranger is usually met with an undisguised curiousity but it is rarely, if ever, hostile. The fact that so many aspects of Portuguese life have remained apparently untouched by the twentieth century is partially a result of the Salazar years. Between 1933 and 1974 Portugal was governed by a right-wing dictatorship which suppressed all opposition and largely failed to stimulate internal economic growth through over-reliance on its increasingly rebellious colonies. Modernisation of the infrastructure was limited, so that, even today, there is no continuous motorway between the country's two major towns, Lisbon and Oporto.

For the tourist, this ossification means that much of the country has remained 'unspoilt', but for many Portuguese it has meant poverty so extreme that the only alternative has been emigration. When the revolution came in 1974, the promise of land reform was highly popular but the ensuing nationalisation improved conditions but not productivity.

Nostalgia for former, better times is part of what is meant by the word *saudade*, but it can also refer to a more general pessimism, a self-conscious romantic melancholy, splendidly depicted in Eça de Queiroz's great novel, *The Maias*. It is this fatalism which supposedly most distinguishes the Portuguese from their neighbours in Spain and it is most directly expressed in the plaintive music of the Lisbon *fado*, songs of love and death performed with almost unbearable pathos. But in a country that has recently joined the European Community and is at last beginning to abandon its sense of insularity, perhaps this is one national myth that could usefully be laid to rest.

Getting to Portugal

If you are from an EC country, North America or Australia you need a passport to enter Portugal, but a visa is not necessary unless you are from New Zealand or intend to stay more than two months.

There is no direct **ferry** link between Britain and Portugal but there is one run by Brittany Ferries (0752 221 321), between Britain (Plymouth) and Northern Spain (Santander). It takes about 24 hours and runs twice a week during the holiday season. A **train** leaves London (Victoria) for Lisbon (Santa Apolonia Station) everyday, via Paris and Irun. The journey takes about 36 hours. If you drive to Paris by car, you can use the **motorail** service between Paris and Lisbon.

Lisbon, Oporto and Faro are Portugal's main **airports**. There are many scheduled direct flights to choose from, whereas cheap charter flights tend to be available only out of season. Air Portugal (TAP) leaves from London (Heathrow) for all three destinations, as well as from Manchester for Lisbon and Oporto. British Airways flies from London (Gatwick) to all three destinations.

Car hire is quite expensive if you make your arrangements in Portugal, so it is worth investigating some of the fly-drive schemes offered by travel agents. Driving all the way from one of the French channel ports is another option but the distance is about 2,000km.

Roads and Maps

If you are not in a hurry, you will probably find Portugal's roads are not as bad as you may expect. True, the main route from Lisbon to Oporto is only sporadically a motorway (at other times it thins down, literally, into a village high street) and on more than one main road we saw traffic held up by the crossing of a shepherd and his flock. Generally our routes keep to small country roads, where particular care should be exercised, since ox-drawn carts and donkeys are still common methods of transport and many people simply travel on foot.

Since Portugal joined the EC, there has been a marked increase in new roads and improvement of old ones, particularly in the north. This means that maps and road numbers can become out of date quite quickly, even the reliable Michelin map for Portugal (No. 437) which is the one we used and recommend. Maps of greater detail can be obtained in Lisbon, in offices next to the Estrela church, but most of these are over 20 years old.

Driving

To drive in Portugal, you need an international driving licence and (for insurance cover equal to what you have at home) a 'green card' from your insurance company. The wearing of seat belts is compulsory and, in the event of an accident or breakdown, a red warning triangle must be displayed. It is worth being a member of the AA or the RAC since both have an arrangement with the **ACP (Automóvel Clube de Portugal)** if you ever need assistance. Their headquarters are in the Rua Rosa Araújo in Lisbon (01 563 931, or 01 775 402 for emergencies) and there are branches in Oporto, Aveiro, Braga, Coimbra and Faro.

In the remoter regions, petrol stations keep limited hours and are often few and far between, so it is advisable to fill up your tank when you can; do not assume that credit cards will be accepted everywhere. Driving is on the right; the speed limits are 60kmph in built-up areas and 90kmph elsewhere, except on motorways, where it is 120kmph. Portuguese drivers have an even worse reputation than the roads. Unfortunately, it is very much more justified, with Portugal possessing the worst record in Europe for accidents. Emergency services can be summoned by telephoning 115.

Accommodation

Pousadas are the grandest and most expensive places to stay: state-run hotels, the equivalent of Spanish *Paradores*, they are usually beautifully located, often in an historical building such as an old convent, a castle or a palace. There are 30 throughout Portugal and it is advisable to book ahead through the *pousada* organisation **ENATUR** in Lisbon (01 8481 221).

Many of Portugal's most beautiful, privately-owned country houses may be visited only if you wish to stay in them. Several of these are in the Minho region, often in the heart of some of the lushest countryside. The scheme is called **Turismo de Habitação** and includes some less grandiose private houses, which are correspondingly cheaper. Bookings and further details can be obtained from the **Associação das Casas do Turismo de Habitação** (01 284 2901).

The prices of hotels vary enormously and reflect the popularity of an area. Hotels in Lisbon and the Algarve are usually more expensive than anywhere else. A hotel has a higher status than a pension (*pensão*) but will not necessarily be superior. It is always worth shopping around and, unless you are in a popular place in high season, booking is not usually necessary. The tariff, giving the maximum and minimum charges, should be attached to the back of each bedroom door. If there are two of you, then having a single room (*um quarto simples*) each is always more expensive than sharing a double room (*um duplo*). A room with a double bed is called *um quarto de casal*.

A *residencial* is much the same as a *pensão* but an *estalagem* or *albergaria* is more like a three- or four-star inn. An alternative to all of these, particularly if everywhere seems full, is to hire a room in a private house. Enquire at the local Tourist Office or at a *pensão* and there is usually someone who knows someone else with a room to rent.

Camping

An even cheaper option is to camp. There are over 100 camp sites in the country, most of them of a high standard and some, like the one in the Monsanto Park near Lisbon (01 708 384), positively luxurious. Prices are reduced out of season and an International Camping Card will get you a discount at some sites. Specific sites will be mentioned throughout the book but for further details write to **Federação Portuguesa de Campismo e Caravanismo**, Rua da Vaz do Operario I, 1100 Lisboa (01 862 350).

Eating and Drinking

Food

Portuguese cooking is simple and wholesome and usually comes in enormous portions. There are many regional differences and specialities but, on the whole, the same standard dishes reappear throughout the country. Even away from the coast, fish (*peixe*) predominates and the nearest thing to a national dish is *bacalhau* (dried salt cod) though most of it seems to be imported from Norway. There is said to be a different way of cooking *bacalhau* for every day of the year, so make sure you know exactly what you are getting, as many recipes are an acquired taste. *Bacalhau com natas* (creamed) and *bacalhau a brás* (with eggs and potatoes) are very popular. Equally ubiquitous are *sardinhas* (sardines), which you can often buy ready to eat from charcoal grills set up on the street. Fish tends to be served with boiled potatoes (*batatas cozidas*) and a salad (*salada*), if you ask for it. Green vegetables as a side dish are not common.

Meat (*carne*) is usually served with chips (*batatas fritas*). Portugal does not have much grazing land and beef (*carne da vaca* or *bife*) and veal (*vitela*) may be tough. Pork (*porco*) and chicken (*frango*) are more reliable. In the country, lamb (*anho* or *borrego*) is common, as are goat (*cabra*) and kid (*cabrito*), though where the latter is listed on the menu, you whould watch out for elderly imitations.

It is perfectly acceptable for two people to share a main dish (*uma dose*) or to ask for a half portion (*uma meia dose*). With a soup (*sopa*) and a dessert (*sombremesa*) this can be filling enough. Soups include the famous *caldo verde* from the Minho, made from finely chopped cabbage, and *sopa à alentejana*, a garlic soup with egg and bread in it. There are four more or less standard desserts: *pudim flan* or simply, *flan*, (crème caramel), *arroz-doce* (rice pudding), *mousse de chocolate* (chocolate mousse) and the mysterious *molotov* (a kind of soufflé).

Breakfast (*pequeno almoço*) tends to be simple, usually bread (*pãe*) or rolls (*pãezinhos*) and coffee. Times of main meals are quite strictly adhered to. Lunch (*almoço*) is from 12 noon to 3pm but do not arrive after 2.45pm. Dinner (*janta*) is more varied, the peak time is about 8pm but several times in the country we found all the restaurants closed by 9pm. Service is usually included in the bill (*a conta*) but a small tip will be appreciated.

The greatest culinary inventiveness (in some cases traceable to the old monastic kitchens) seems reserved for the making of cakes and pastries. These are consumed, with great relish and at all times of the day, at cake-selling bars or cafes called (*pastelarias*). They are much less light and creamy than French pastries, tending to be eggy, heavy and sometimes very sweet.

Drink

Coffee drinking is a serious occupation in Portugal and the coffee comes in many forms. *Uma bica* is a small, strong black coffee, like an espresso. With a drop of milk it is called *uma pingada* and when slightly diluted, *uma bica cheia*. In the north, *uma bica* is called *um café*. A small white coffee is *um garoto* and a larger white coffee *uma meia de leite* (half of milk), the nearest equivalent to what passes for a cup of coffee in England. *Um galão* is a large tumbler almost filled with milk, which is then frothed up and a *bica* added. There is a deluxe version, *um galão da maquina*, which makes the perfect breakfast drink.

There are many natural springs and spas in Portugal and so plenty of inexpensive mineral waters to choose from. In restaurants or bars, you ask for *água mineral*, either *com gas* (fizzy) or *sem gas* (still), and you can specify temperature, *frio* (cool) or *natural* (room temperature). It is perfectly safe to drink tap water, although it tends to be quite heavily chlorinated.

Port, a major Portuguese product of which large quantities are exported to the UK, is a dessert wine made from grapes grown in the Upper Douro Valley and fortified with brandy. In the spring, after harvest, it is taken down river to Oporto where it is stored at the great wine lodges in wooden casks. An outstanding year will be declared a vintage and left to mature, without any additions, for as long as 20 years. However, the majority of ports are a blended mixture of wines from different years. Of these, ruby port, full and sweet, is the most popular, even though it is matured for the shortest period. Tawny port is aged longer, is less sweet and has altogether a more subtle taste, while the white port, gradually increasing in popularity, is usually chilled and drunk as an aperitif.

There are many excellent, and astonishingly inexpensive, table wines, few of which are well known outside Portugal apart from Mateus Rosé and Lancers, wines not taken very seriously in Portugal. In fact, in recent years, the *vinhos verdes* or 'green wines' from the Minho have become better known. The 'green' refers not to their colour but their youth which, with their natural effervescence and low alcohol content, makes them an excellent summer wine when chilled. Whites are more popular but the reds are just as good, particularly if drunk near their place of origin, since neither wine travels well.

Most of the country's wine-making takes place in the north but there are a total of ten officially demarcated regions throughout the country, all of which employ markedly different methods of viticulture. This process of demarcation was begun by the Marquis of Pombal in 1756 to regulate the industry and to stop irregularities in wine production. Unfortunately, several of these regions, especially those round Lisbon, have become very small and run the risk of being completely swallowed up by urban encroachment.

Health

It is advisable to take out health insurance since there is no free medical treatment for tourists in Portugal. For assistance with minor ailments visit the chemist (*farmácia*), open during normal shopping hours, where advice and treatment will be of a high professional standard. Out of hours, you will find a list on the door detailing the nearest available night service. Many doctors and chemists speak good English. Emergency services can be summoned by telephoning 115.

Telephones and Post

Phoning long distance from public kiosks is difficult unless you find one that takes a phone card. Using the post office (*correio*) is a more reliable method but they are often crowded and only open Monday to Friday from 9am to 6pm (the exceptions are the main Lisbon and Oporto branches). If you phone from a hotel or bar, a dial will indicate the number of units you are using but a substantial surcharge is always added.

Post restante mail can be sent to any post office in Portugal. As well as carrying the recipient's name and the address of the post office, the envelope should be marked *Lista da Correios*. Passport identification is needed to collect the mail.

Tourist Information

The Portuguese National Tourist Board is an indispensible source of up to date information and travel ideas. The main office in Lisbon is in the **Palácio Foz**, Praça dos Restauradores (363 3314/3643). All main towns have tourist offices (*turismo*) which are worth visiting for more detailed local information, maps, lists of sites, festivals, times of openings, etc., even though these are often translated into a barely comprehensible English.

Main Offices abroad:
22–25a Sackville Street, London W1X 1DE (071 494 1441)
548 Fifth Avenue, New York NY 10036 (212 354 4403)

Public Holidays

1 January	New Year
Shrove Tuesday	(known as *Carnaval* or *Entrudo*)
Good Friday	
25 April	Liberty Day (commemorating the Revolution of 1974)
1 May	Labour Day
25 May	Corpus Christi
10 June	Portugal Day (death of Camões, the national poet)
15 August	Assumption of the Virgin
5 October	Republic Day (its founding in 1910)
1 November	All Saints Day
1 December	Restoration of Independence (from Spain in 1640)
8 December	The Immaculate Conception
25 December	Christmas

St Anthony's day (13 June) is celebrated in Lisbon and St John the Baptist's day (25 June) in Oporto. Several other towns have their own special days—for details check with the local tourist office.

Background Information

The Land

The type of ownership and management of the land varies from region to region but the most obvious difference is between the north and the south as a whole. The south, particularly the Alentejo, is made up of vast individually owned estates (*latifundios*) formerly employing workers on a seasonal basis to farm the land. North of Lisbon, the pattern is one of individually-owned small-holdings (*minifundios*) geared towards self-sufficiency. Crudely speaking, this means that the south has always been more politicised, with a history of anti-clericism, whereas the north tends to be conservative and much more religious.

When the revolution came in 1974, many of the big landowners in the Alentejo fled and their were lands occupied by the workers. This was legalised by the Agrarian Reform Law of 1975, which established the farms as workers' cooperatives. Whatever the success of these and despite the obviously improved conditions of employment, these land reforms have gradually been whittled away by subsequent governments and, in many cases, the lands have been returned to their former owners.

In the north, the smallholders' reluctance to change has made it difficult to carry out a long-term agricultural policy. A relatively recent idea has been the mass planting of eucalpytus trees, largely to benefit the growing paper industry. These trees grow quickly but adversely affect the soil as well as transforming the appearance of the landscape. Their planting has general met with enthusiasm but there has been strong resistance, in the form of demonstrations and, even the deliberate starting of forest fires, when common land has been taken over.

The Church

Portugal is a devoutly Catholic country and, despite the gradual erosion of its power, the Church still exerts a strong influence over the lives of many people. The shrine of Our Lady of Fátima is evidence of this. Founded on the site where three children claimed to have seen the Virgin Mary sitting in a holm oak tree in May 1917, it is now one of the most important Marian shrines in Europe and the scene of massive pilgrimages, particularly on 13 May and 13 October, the first and the last dates of the children's six visions. Many people, often quite poor, wish to make the pilgrimage at least once in their lives, either in thanks for God's blessing or in the hope of it. On the two special days the roads near Fátima are filled with people who have walked for many miles, sometimes on their knees for the final stages.

Fátima is only the most famous and extreme manifestation of the local festivals of popular saints, called *romarias*, which exist up and down the country. Nearly every town and village claims a special relationship with a saint who is often endowed with a highly implausible set of attributes (probably unconnected with his or her historical reality). The saint's task is to protect and unite the local community. The festivals around the saint's day are often prolonged and lavish, and many of the shrines are magnificent churches, embellished over the centuries by donations from the pilgrims.

The monastic tradition was immensely strong and unusually long-lived in Portugal. In 1760, the Marquis of Pombal briefly curtailed the monks' wealth and power when he disbanded the monasteries and sold off their properties. When the insane, but highly devout, Maria I came to the throne, she simply gave them back and it was not until 1838 that they were finally and irrevocably closed down. Many quite small towns, like Arouca, are dominated by huge monastic foundations which have fallen into disrepair or been taken over by the local council and turned into museums.

Historical links with the UK

A brief summary of Portuguese history is given in the Chronology on pp. 114–18, but links with the UK have had such a strong influence on Portuguese history and culture that they merit a special note here.

England and Portugal claim the longest surviving alliance in Europe, one established by treaties in 1373 and 1386. In fact, relations go back even earlier than that and arguably they have been more to Britain's advantage than to Portugal's.

Anglo-Norman crusaders helped the first Portuguese king, Afonso Henriques, recapture Lisbon from the Moors in 1147. An English priest, Gilbert of Hastings, became the city's new bishop and then did much to enlist support from his native land as the continuing reconquest advanced to the south.

The Duke of Lancaster, John of Gaunt, supported the claims of João of Avis to the Portuguese throne and a small contingent of English archers fought at the decisive Battle of Aljubarrota in 1385. As king, Dom João I cemented the relationship with the English by the Treaty of Windsor in 1386 and by marrying Philippa of Lancaster (John of Gaunt's daughter) the following year.

A less successful marriage was secured, between Catherine of Bragança and the English king Charles II by a treaty in 1661. The English gained the Portuguese colonies of Bombay and Tangier but the couple had no children and Catherine returned to Portugal shortly after Charles's death.

1703 saw the more significant Methuen Treaty negotiated. In return for special conditions for the import of British manufactured goods, the Portuguese secured a market in Britain for their agricultural produce (especially wine). This was ultimately detrimental to the development of Portugal's own industrial base. It certainly helped to consolidate the port trade but, even at this date, the industry was practically run by the British anyway.

The help given by the British army and Wellington in ridding Portugal of Napoleon's troops between 1807 and 1811 was more than repaid when the country effectively became a British protectorate. A former officer of Wellington's, Marshal Beresford, governed the country in the absence of the Royal family until 1821. The war also resulted in trade with Brazil being opened up to Britain.

Later in the century, when Portuguese and British interests clashed in Africa, Britain simply laid down the law. In 1887, a plan to link Angola and Mozambique was prevented by an ultimatum from the British Prime Minister, Lord Salisbury. Eight years later, Britain and Germany were secretly planning to divide up Portugal's African empire between them.

During the Second World War, Salazar, the Portuguese Prime Minister, pursued a highly expedient foreign policy. Under the guise of neutrality, Portugal sold wolfram (an ore containing tungsten) to the Germans but in 1943 permitted the Allies to have vitally important bases in the Azores.

Glossary

adega	wine cellar or winery
alcaide	Arabic word, retained after the reconquest, meaning the military governor of a city or town
aldeia	village
armillary sphere	a sketetal model of the celestial sphere used for navigational purposes. Adopted by Dom Manuel I as his personal emblem and later incorporated into the Portuguese coat-of-arms.
azulejo	glazed decorative tile, often blue and white, employed on the inside and outside of buildings. Originally made by Arabs and imported from Seville, they were manufactured in Portugal by the end of the sixteenth century.
bairro	district of a town
barragem	dam
capela-mór	chancel and sanctuary of a church
castro	fortified, Iron Age hill-town
chafariz	public fountain
colheita	year or vintage of a wine
converso	Jew (forcibly) converted to Christianity
convento	convent
Cortes	medieval parliament
Descobrimentos	the Discoveries, a collective term for the achievements of the great Portuguese explorers (Vasco da Gama, Diogo Cão, *et al*) during the sixteenth century.
Dom, Dona	male and female courtesy titles, used only on very formal occasions. The Portuguese refer to their kings and queens by these titles.
espigueiro	storehouse for grain or corn, standing on mushroom-shaped legs to keep out vermin. Found in the Minho region and in Galicia in Spain.
Estado Novo	the New State. Name of the fascist regime which controlled Portugal from 1926 to 1974.
fado(s)	intensely melancholic song(s), possibly derived from North African music, performed with great emotion by a singer and guitarist(s)
feriado/festa	holiday/festival

foral	charter given by the king to a town or city setting out its rights and privileges
grutas	caves
igreja	church
igreja matriz	parish church
Judiaria	Jewish quarter or ghetto
largo	small town square
maduro	matured wine
Manueline	an elaborate, and uniquely Portuguese, late expression of the Gothic in architecture. It lasted longer than the reign of Dom Manuel I (1495–1521), after whom it is named, and contains intricately carved decorative motifs (twisted rope, coral, exotic fruits) inspired by the Discoveries.
marrano	(lit: swine) term of abuse used against Jews forcibly converted to Christianity, many of whom continued to practice their faith in secret, and who now refer to themselves defiantly as marranos
mosteiro	monastery
Moor	generic term for all the Muslim invaders and occupants of the Iberian peninsula
Mouraria	moorish quarter
Mozarab	Christian under Moorish subjection (also applied to architecture)
Mudejar	Muslim under Christian subjection (also applied to architecture)
PCP	(Partido Comunista Portugues) Portuguese Communist Party
PIDE	(Polícia International e de Defesa do Estado) Salazar's Secret Police
PS	(Partido Socialista) Socialist Party
PSD	(Partido Social-Democrata) Social Democratic Party
paço	palace
pelourinho	stone column, ostensibly a pillory but really serving as a symbol of municipal authority, usually situated in the town's main square and often decorated
pensão	inexpensive accommodation, usually with food
pousada	state-run luxury hotel
praça	large town square
praia	beach
quinta	country house and its estate
romaria	rural pilgrimage and festival, held annually on the local patron saint's day
saudade	a peculiarly Portuguese idea suggesting an unspecific yearning for what was and is no more; an institutionalised melancholy encapsulated by *fado*.
Sé	cathedral (or See)
serra	mountain or mountain range

solar	northern equivalent of *quinta*
talha dourada	gilded woodwork, especially the spectacular baroque altarpieces found in many churches
Templar	military religious order established for the protection of pilgrims to the Holy Land and active in the Christian reconquest of the peninsula.
torre de menagem	main tower or keep of a castle

Metric Conversion Tables

All measurements are given in metric units. For readers more familiar with the imperial system, the accompanying tables are for quick conversion to metric units. Bold figures in the central columns can be read as either metric or imperial: e.g. 1kg = 2.20lb or 1lb = 0.45kg.

mm		in	cm		in	m		yds
25.4	1	.039	2.54	1	0.39	0.91	1	1.09
50.8	2	.079	5.08	2	0.79	1.83	2	2.19
76.2	3	.118	7.62	3	1.18	2.74	3	3.28
101.6	4	.157	10.16	4	1.57	3.66	4	4.37
127.0	5	.197	12.70	5	1.97	4.57	5	5.47
152.4	6	.236	15.24	6	2.36	5.49	6	6.56
177.8	7	.276	17.78	7	2.76	6.40	7	7.66
203.2	8	.315	20.32	8	3.15	7.32	8	8.75
228.6	9	.354	22.86	9	3.54	8.23	9	9.84

g		oz	kg		lb	km		miles
28.35	1	.04	0.45	1	2.20	1.61	1	0.62
56.70	2	.07	0.91	2	4.41	3.22	2	1.24
85.05	3	.11	1.36	3	6.61	4.83	3	1.86
113.40	4	.14	1.81	4	8.82	6.44	4	2.48
141.75	5	.18	2.27	5	11.02	8.05	5	3.11
170.10	6	.21	2.72	6	13.23	9.65	6	3.73
198.45	7	.25	3.18	7	15.43	11.26	7	4.35
226.80	8	.28	3.63	8	17.64	12.87	8	4.97
255.15	9	.32	4.08	9	19.84	14.48	9	5.59

ha		acres
0.40	1	2.47
0.81	2	4.94
1.21	3	7.41
1.62	4	9.88
2.02	5	12.36
2.43	6	14.83
2.83	7	17.30
3.24	8	19.77
3.64	9	22.24

Metric to imperial conversion formulae:

	multiply by
cm to inches	0.3937
m to feet	3.281
m to yards	1.094
km to miles	0.6214
km to square miles	0.3861
ha to acres	2.471
g to ounces	0.03527
kg to pounds	2.205

1 ESTREMADURA

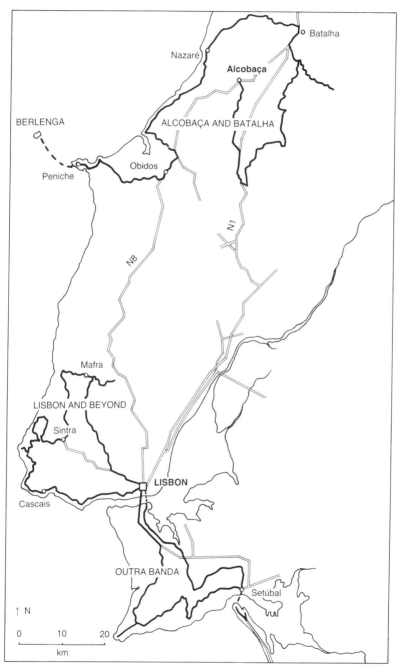

Batalha

Nazaré

Alcobaça

BERLENGA

ALCOBAÇA AND BATALHA

Obidos

Peniche

N1

N8

Mafra

LISBON AND BEYOND

Sintra

LISBON

Cascais

OUTRA BANDA

Setúbal

↑ N

| 0 | 10 | 20 |

km

When Portugal became a kingdom in 1139, the province now known as Estremadura was still occupied by the Moors. Dom Afonso Henriques, determined to extend his territories southwards, captured Santarém and Lisbon in 1147. The area laid waste by these continuous struggles was recultivated, partially by Crusader settlers but mainly by Cistercian monks and, in 1260, Dom Afonso III transferred his court to Lisbon and made it his new capital. Though small, Estremadura is a province of great variety with the fertile fruit-growing valleys near Alcobaça lying close to the dry Candeeiros mountains. Its coastline has provided fisherman with a hard and dangerous way of life over many centuries and the presence of several coastal fortresses shows that the threat was from pirates and other marauders as well as from the sea itself. There is an abundance of outstanding monuments, including four royal palaces, as well as the two great monasteries at Batalha and Alcobaça. All this has long made it very popular with English visitors: Lord Byron, William Beckford and Robert Southey all more or less concentrated their travels on this region around the capital.

Lisbon and Beyond

3 days/140km/from Lisbon

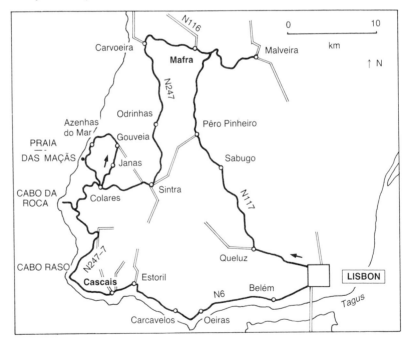

Beginning an exploration of rural Portugal in Lisbon may seem odd but is justifiable by its proximity to the countryside and also simply because it is one of the least known but most beautiful of all European cities, in spite of much unnecessary demolition over the last ten years.

To the north the Serra de Sintra, with its forests and cool breezes, provides the perfect antidote to the bustle and grime of a city in summer. Such has been its appeal, over the centuries, for those rich enough to build manor houses and palaces there and today its continued popularity has not managed to destroy its charms.

LISBON (Lisboa) pop: 2,100,000 including suburbs. The most spectacular approach to the city is from across the River Tagus (Tejo), either over the '25 April' suspension bridge or by ferry from Cacilhas. When Henry Fielding came here for his health in 1754, he thought it 'the nastiest city in the world'. He died a few months later and the following year the city was almost totally destroyed by a devastating earthquake, which killed at least 13,000 people and left many more homeless. It was rebuilt, on strictly rational lines, by the all-powerful Chief Minister, the Marquis of Pombal, and its centre has remained relatively unchanged since then.

Moving north from the main ferry stop (Terreiro do Paço), over land reclaimed from the river, takes you through a great arcaded square, the Praça de Comercio, with its bronze equestrian statue of Dom José I in the middle and, on its north side, a large triumphal arch with statues of Pombal and Vasco da Gama. Immediately to the north of this lies a regular grid of busy commercial streets known as the Baixa (low district) which leads to two adjacent squares; the Rossio (or Praça de Dom Pedro IV—he is in the middle on a column) and the Praça da Figueira with another equestrian statue, this time of Dom João I. At a booth, at the corner of this square, you can buy a weekly travel pass, which allows the use of buses, metro, trams and funiculars. Taxis—black with green roofs—are plentiful and cheap.

On from the Rossio, past the National Theatre and the main station, leads you into yet another 'square', the Praça dos Restaurodores, named after the conspirators who successfully restored Portuguese independence by overthrowing their Spanish rulers in 1640. On the left is the eighteenth-century Palaçio Foz, part of which now houses the main **Tourist Office**. The square also marks the beginning of Lisbon's largest thoroughfare, the Avenida da Liberdade, which rises gently for about half a mile before culminating in the rather grandiose monument to Pombal, erected in 1934.

Two hills rising up on either side of the old centre of town contain, to the west, the **Bairro Alto** (high district) and, to the east, the old Moorish quarter of the Alfama, crowned by the much restored **castle of São Jorge**. The Bairro Alto can be reached by funicular from Restaurodores (calçada de Gloria) or by the Eiffel-designed lift in the Rua Santa Justa (elevador de Santa Justa) or you can walk via the fashionable shops of the old Chiado area (Rua do Carmo and Rua Garrett), disastrously reduced by fire in 1988.

The **Alfama**, a dense and confusing network of narrow, bustling streets and connecting steps, feels like a different, decidedly non-European city. On Tuesday and Saturday mornings, a large street market (the Feira da Ladra) sprawls out behind the magnificent Renaissance church of São

Lisbon's coat of arms

Vicente de Fora. Both these districts are good places for hearing *fado* but their darkest and narrowest streets should be avoided at night, especially if alone.

The city has several museums, including the gloomy **Museu de Arte Antiga** in Rua Janelas Verdas, which contains the national collection; the fine **Muzeu Azulejo**, incorporating the extraordinarily ornate church of Madre de Deus; and the famous collection of the Gulbenkian Foundation in the Avenida Berna. The latter is part of a large arts complex, set in a sculpture park to the north of the city, just beyond the large, but unexciting, Parque Eduardo VII (the English King visited Lisbon in 1903). There are other smaller, more intimate parks and gardens; within the São Jorge Castle; opposite the great Baroque Estrela church (next to the English cemetery where Fielding is buried); and, best of all, the lush and mysterious Botanical Garden off the Rua Escola Politecnica—a small forest of palms set on a hill—cool in summer, sheltered in winter.

The emblem of the city, visible everywhere, on lamp-posts, pavement designs, even on dustbins, is a stylised single-sailed ship with a raven at each end. This represents the journey, in 1173, of the remains of São Vicente (Saint Vincent, the pensinsula's first martyr and the patron saint of the city) from Cape St Vincent, in the Algarve, to his final resting place in Lisbon, guided and watched over by a flock of ravens.

There are many places to stay in Lisbon, and we recommend two of them. **The Pensão Casa de São Mamede** (663 166) is comfortable and well situated near the Botanical Gardens. The **Pensão Ninho de Aguias** (862 591), by the Castle walls, is less plush but possesses a fantastic view of both river and city.

If you are driving from central Lisbon, find your way to the Rato district and then follow the signs for **Sintra**. This will take you past the monstrous post-modern shopping centre of Amoreiras (of which Lisboetas seem unduly proud), past the great eighteenth-century Aqueduct of Águas Livres (free waters) and onto the motorway to Sintra. This takes you through part of the Monsanto Park and, not long after, you can see in the distance the Serra de Sintra, topped by the Palácio da Pena (see p.20).

The right-hand turning for **QUELUZ** appears quite suddenly and almost immediately you are in front of the rose-stuccoed Royal Palace, in whose front courtyard stands a statue of the mad Queen, Dona Maria I, gazing gloomily across at the barracks and bell-tower on the other side of the road. The building of the palace took place over a 45-year period, beginning in 1747. It was initially planned as a small summer residence for the Infante Dom Pedro (later Pedro III) but when he married his niece, Dona Maria (the heir to the throne) the French architect, J.B. Robillion, was employed to enlarge it. The result is a discreet mix of the Rococo and the Classical, a little unprepossessing from the road, but when seen in combination with the parterred formal gardens and their statues and fountains, the effect is elegant and inventive.

A relaxed guided tour of the interior includes the magnificently ornate throne-room and the more restrained music room (still used for public concerts), the grandiose but damaged Ambassador's room and its ante-chamber, the Corridor of Sleeves, decorated with blue and yellow *azulejos*. If you visit in the morning, a good but expensive lunch can be had at the restaurant in the former kitchens, called, appropriately, **Cozinha Velha** (The Old Kitchen) (950 740).

From here, to head north for another Royal residence, the palace-convent at Mafra, you should turn right and continue into town, then turn left, go past the railway station and onto the N117 for Belas. Though close to Lisbon, this is surprisingly unspoilt and beautiful countryside.

The inhabitants of the territory to the immediate north and west of Lisbon are called *Saloios*. Their precise origin is unknown but they may have been *Cristão-novos* (new Christians) — that is forcibly converted Jews — who left Lisbon to escape persecution. By tradition they supplied the capital with agricultural produce while the women, known as *lavadeiras*, would collect laundry and wash it in the streams with ashes before returning it by donkey to Lisbon.

Continue through the village of Sabugo, from where you can still see the palace of Pena to your left, and on through Pero Pinheiro, whose famous quarries produce a pinkish marble, notably employed in the church of Mafra's palace-convent some 13km to the north.

The road divides at the junction with the N116 — almost within sight of the convent — and, if it is a Thursday, it is worth turning right and making a detour to **MALVEIRA**, where there is an excellent weekly market, selling mostly agricultural produce but also much else, including pots and clothes. It is also a good place to stop for good cheap country food.

If not making this detour, follow the N116 to your left and soon you will see the turrets of the **MAFRA** palace peeping out from behind the hills. This approach, sliding in from the side, gives you no real sense of the scale of the whole building, which is huge and appeared to Beckford '. . . like a vast street of palaces'. Built on a square plan and covering 80sq m (850 sq ft) the front, with the church in the centre, contains the palace, whilst the rest of it was for the use of the monks. They were Franciscans from Arrábida, rehoused by Dom João V (whose religious devotions included a rather unspiritual interest in young nuns), in thanks for their successful prediction of the Queen's pregnancy. By the time work on the building started in 1717, Dona Ana-Maria had already produced three children, and the plans for the monastery (which were originally for a mere 13 monks) became much more ambitious. Expense was not spared: the seemingly endless riches of Brazil provided the cash and some of the materials, and the size of the project kept on increasing. At one point, in the rush to complete the basilica, over 50,000 people were at work.

The result of this absolutist *folie de grandeur*, which practically bankrupt the country, looks formidable but not entirely convincing. 'I cannot pretend that the style of the building is such as a Roman or English architect would approve,' was Beckford's verdict. It looks as though it was designed by a committee, although the principal architect was the German, Johann Ludwig (João Ludovice), who had first-hand experience of the Roman Baroque, which the building most resembles.

The three-storey front, anchored at either end by squat pavilions with unusual canopied domes, is long and monotonous. The portico of the basilica is surmounted by two tall towers containing between them a carillon of 114 bells, which can be heard on the first Sunday of each month. Entering the church, through a vestibule filled with a dramatic array of sculptured saints, again the impression is of great size and wealth rather than inspiration, and of coldness, despite the use of a wide range of different coloured marbles.

The church may be visited independently but, to see more, the visitor is given a rapid one-hour tour of a mere ten per cent of the building. Of the rest, 85 per cent is occupied by the army and five per cent by the municipality. Of all the rooms (royal apartments, monks' cells, infirmary, kitchens) the outstanding one is the long, galleried library: barrel vaulted, with a dome in the middle and decorated in a restrained Baroque style, it contains over 30,000 volumes.

The last King of Portugal, Dom Manuel II, spent his final days here before exile to England in 1910, but generally it was little used by the Royal Family. During the Peninsular War, both the French General Junot and the Duke of Wellington used it, at different times, as their military headquarters.

Emerging from the building after an hour or so is a shock; everything seems out of scale; the town looks like a toy. There is not much else here except soldiers, a rather run-to-seed park behind the palace and, at the bottom of the town, a small, medieval church, which was closed when we visited.

Continue northwards (past the front of the monastery) and just after leaving town, turn left for Carvoeira. Here, turn left again onto the N247, which leads to Sintra. The retrospective views of the monastery, particularly along this road, make it look more beautiful and less formidable than it does close up. At the village of **ODRINHAS**, there is a small archaeological museum, set in the ruins of a Roman villa, where you can see a good mosaic floor and a large collection of Roman epigraphs.

After about another 15km, **SINTRA**, which has been visible for some time, is finally reached. This is one of Portugal's most celebrated resorts and one about which many visitors (in particular the English) have waxed eloquent. Lord Byron, who stayed here in 1809, called it 'glorious Eden' and thought it wasted on the Portuguese, but the most romantic account of its beauty is in Chapter 8 of Eça de Queiroz's novel, *The Maias*

> . . . he gazed down in wonder at the immense wealth of dense trees clothing one slope of the mountain the way lichen covers a wall, and at that distance seeming in the brilliant light as soft and smooth as a blanket of dark-green moss.

It lives up to its reputation. Despite the coach parties and the tourist shops, the whole area of the Serra de Sintra possesses a magical beauty. This is partly because of its mild, moist climate, which produces verdure of great lushness and variety, but also because its self-containment makes it seem like your own vast yet secret garden.

This must have been the great attraction for Dom João I who built the **Paço Real**, or Royal Palace, here as his summer residence in the early fifteenth century. It still dominates the centre of town with its huge conical twin chimneys protruding into the sky. These date from the eighteenth century and, indeed, the whole of the palace is an odd but satisfying jumble of styles. The ornate windows are thought to have come originally from Venice via Ceuta, following the latter's occupation by Portugal in 1415. There are also many Manueline details, notably the doors and windows inside the long Sala dos Cisnes, named after the 27 swans with golden collars that decorate its ceiling. This room also contains a dado and window surrounds of green-and-white tiles and, as a whole, the palace provides an anthology of *azulejos*, including some of the earliest, on the floor of the chapel. This, of course, reflects the Moorish influence, which is very strong, not just in the detailing but also in the several cool and quiet rooms and courtyards, such as the exquisitely simple Sala dos Arabes.

The Royal Palace at Sintra

The successful conquest of Ceuta, which instigated Portuguese imperialism, was planned here by Dom João and his sons, as was the disastrous African campaign of Dom Sebastião, which effectively ended imperial expansion in 1578. You are taken round the palace by a tour guide, the immediate post-luncheon tour being probably the least frenetic. The palace is closed on Wednesdays.

Nearby, in the Largo da Republica, is the **Tourist Office**, which will supply you with a map of the town and surroundings and advise you about hotels. We stayed at the **Pensão Sintra** (923 0738), up towards São Pedro, which was very pretty, good value and had the advantage of being away from the main tourist bustle in the middle of town. At the extreme end of the spectrum in terms of luxury and expense is the **Palácio de Seteais** (923 3200/25), once a private house and now a grand hotel worth visiting even if you are not planning to stay there, though even a soft drink will set you back. The left hand buildings were erected in the 1780s for a Dutch diamond merchant. The triumphal arch and right-hand wing were added later by the house's next owner, the Marquis of Marialva. The arch opens onto a terrace with a magnificent view and the popular explanation of the house's unusual name is that a shout of 'ai' will be echoed seven (*sete*) times around the valley.

Seteais is close to **Monserrate** and on the same road. These two are the only Quintas in Sintra easily accessible to the public but they are two of the finest and marvellously contrasted. Seteais has a simple neo-classical gravity, whereas Monserrate is one of the most poignant and romantic sites in the whole of Portugal.

In 1811, Byron described it as 'the most desolate mansion in the most beautiful spot I ever beheld'. This was the house built by Gerard de Visme in 1790 and then purchased and rebuilt by Beckford several years later. The house that remains today (though in similarly romantic disrepair) was built for yet another Englishman, Sir Francis Cook, by the architect, James Knowles Sr, in 1860. Stylistically Moorish, it is a wonderfully exotic and original building: long and thin, with a domed pavilion in the centre and two domed towers at each end. The whole house is surrounded by a terrace and you can peer through the windows into the emptiness: the house's contents were sold off in 1948 and only the lavish ornamentation of walls and ceilings survives. But it was really the gardens which made Monserrate famous: romantically lanscaped — there is a ruined chapel — it contains an enormous wealth of tropical plants, and recently work has begun to restore it to a semblance of its former glory.

Sintra contains another monument to the nineteenth-century Romantic imagination, on a grander scale but of a cruder nature, the **Palácio da Pena**. This fantasy castle dominates the Serra for miles around and was the brainchild of Queen Maria II's German-born consort, Dom Fernando II (of the house of Saxe-Coburg Gotha and so a cousin of Prince Albert). On the site of the ruins of yet another Jerónimos monastery, building began in 1840 and stopped only with Dom Fernando's death in 1885. Some parts of the Manueline chapel and a small cloister remain from the original monastery but the rest, even by nineteenth-century standards, is an orgy of excess and fakery, complete with tower and drawbridge; the architect immortalised as a knight in armour; walls lined with porcelain; concrete simulating wood. The views and the large park which surrounds the palace provide a refreshing contrast. The park is large and at its highest point (*cruz alta*) you can see beyond Lisbon to the Serra de Arrábida. On its southern side past the lakes is the Chalé da Condessa, a summer house built by the Countess of Edla who also planted the magnificent surrounding trees. February is an especially good time to visit, when the camellias are in full bloom.

From the Pena Park you can walk down to the much restored **Castelo dos Mouros**, once an important strategic fortification, which changed hands several times between Muslim and Christian. In 1108 passing Norwegian Crusaders, led by Prince Sigurd, captured it but permanent Christian occupation was only achieved by Dom Afonso Henriques in 1147. The ruined chapel of São Pedro, within the castle, dates from this time.

Large parts of Sintra's woods and gardens are private but there are many good walks that connect the main sights. From the Castelo dos Mouros to the Palácio Pena is one, it is also possible to walk from Monserrate to the bizarre **Convento dos Capuchos** in the heart of the woods. This was founded in 1560 for a branch of the Franciscans so ascetic that the convent was actually carved out of the granite rocks of the hills, lined with cork as protection against the damp and minimally decoreated with sea shells. One of its minute cells was occupied by Saint Honorius. The convent is a slightly sinister place, despite the beauty of its surroundings.

On a less frugal note, it is almost impossible to visit Sintra without tasting the local pastry, *queijada*, a kind of cheesecake (one of the reasons for the visit to Sintra as described in *The Maias*). These are sold everywhere, but the best place to try them is at the **Sapa** tea-rooms on the main road into Sintra from Lisbon.

The Fair of São Pedro is on the second and fourth Sundays of each month. Country fare, food, pottery and plants are sold, as well as very over-priced antiques.

Seven km along the N247 through the woods to the west of Sintra is the village of **COLARES**. **The Estalagem do Conde** (929 1652) makes this an alternative to Sintra as a place to stay. The town is pretty enough, with two fine houses, the Quinta do Freixo near the town square and the Quinta Mazziotti higher up the town. Its greatest fame though, derives from what is probably the best red wine in Portugal, produced from vines grown further west on the cliffs near **AZENHAS DO MAR**. The vines are unique, having been planted in sand and so avoiding the great phylloxera epidemic of the 1870s, which devastated vineyards in the rest of Europe. Their maintenance, however, is difficult and laborious: firstly, new vines must be rooted in the clay that lies as much as ten metres beneath the sand (planters wear baskets over their heads to avoid suffocation in the event of the trench collapsing over them); secondly, the vines must be protected from Atlantic winds and sea-water. This is done by training them along the ground and erecting cane palisades as wind-breaks. The result justifies the effort; the wine, usually matured for ten years before it is sold, has a firm, fruity taste, like a good claret but sharper. Unfortunately, the white Colares is not nearly so good.

From here the little village of Penedo is within walking distance, and from Penedo you can also walk up through the forest to the Capuchos monastery, via Bela-Vista.

Heading north from Colares takes you to **JANAS**, where there is an unusual circular church with an equally unusual *romaria*. The church is dedicated to São Mamede, a third century shepherd boy from Caesarea and the patron saint of livestock. Every year on his feast-day, 17 August, the local people assemble with their animals before processing with them three times around the church. Inside, wax ex votos in the shape of cattle can be purchased and placed on the altar and prayers said for sick animals. The present church dates from the sixteenth century but is thought to have been built on the site of a Roman temple.

Continuing north from Janas, the next village is **GOUVEIA**, of no special interest apart from the odd fact that each street bears a poem.

From here we head westwards through the village of Fontanelas before reaching the sea at **AZENHAS DO MAR**, a pretty and relatively unspoilt village that clings to the cliffs. Almost immediately south of it is the **Praia das Maçãs**, one of several beaches between Azenhas do Mar and Cabo Raso. At the height of summer, this and the other larger beaches are packed but it is often possible to find space in the smaller coves just a few minutes' walk away. Even strong and confident swimmers should be careful: the breakers are very powerful and the dragback can easily pull you under. It is also advisable not to leave anything of value in your car if you park on or near the beach. The road (N247) does not follow the coastline here but many of the beaches such as **Praia Grande** and **Praia da Adraga** are reached by small side-roads, the latter via the village of **ALMOÇAGEME**, where there is a good pottery workshop.

A detour via the N247–7 is also needed to reach **Cabo da Roca**, the westernmost point on the continent of Europe, where you can buy a certificate to say as much and that you have been there. Apart from the spectacular views and a lighthouse, there is little else to see and the same is true of Cabo Raso some 10km further south. Between them, however, lies the vast and sandy **Praia do Guincho** and along the road there are several fine seafood restaurants, amongst them the **Raio Verde** (285 9069) and **O Faroleiro** (285 0225).

From here the road, the notorious Estrada Marginal, follows the coast all the way back to Lisbon, through countryside increasingly eroded by development and residential overspill. The famous resorts have boomed but suffered too, although the most famous, **CASCAIS**, still maintains its charm despite the sea being too polluted by Lisbon sewage to swim in. **ESTORIL** is a rich man's ghetto, complete with casino, and at **OEIRAS** is the former Quinta of the Marquis de Pombal. **CARCAVELOS** was once famous for its fortified dessert wine, popular with Wellington's officers, which has now practically disappeared. After this, encroaching Lisbon is a mere 15km away along the N6.

A few kilometres short of Lisbon, you will arrive at **BELÉM** (Bethlehem), worthy of at least a day's visit. It is justly famous for its two great Manueline monuments: the **Tower**, on the water's edge, and the Jerónimos Monastery, about 0.5km inland. Originally the river reached the monastery, and the Tower, built in the early sixteenth century to defend the harbour, was surrounded by water. Francisco de Arruda was responsible for its design and construction, which incorporates Moorish-style balconies, domed look-out posts, and repeated stone shields (used as battlements) bearing the cross of the Order of Christ.

Moving inland along the front you reach, firstly, the **Museu de Arte Popular**, housing a comprehensive collection of traditional Portuguese arts and crafts, and then, a little further along, the highly romantic, if not fascistic, memorial to Henry the Navigator and the seafarers of Portugal. It was from here that the most famous of them all, Vasco da Gama, set sail in 1497 on his fantastic voyage around Africa to India. And it was in thanksgiving for this journey that Dom Manuel ('the Fortunate') founded, and then lavished much wealth and labour on, a new monastery to be occupied by the Jeronymites, a relatively recent order named after Saint Jerome and dedicated to the care of the dying.

The overall conception of the **Jerónimos Monastery** is simple enough but the decorative detailing is immensely rich and imaginative. On the exterior this is mainly concentrated in the south and west portals of which the south is the more extravagant; set between buttresses and tall windows, it is a riot of canopied niches and statuary with a carving of Our Lady of Belém (to whom the church is dedicated) carved above the arch of the door. On the west portal Dom Manuel (with Saint Jerome) and his wife Dona Ana (with John the Baptist) face each other from either side of the door, whilst above them a series of carved tableaux represents the Annuciation, the Nativity and the Adoration of the Magi.

Entering this portal takes you into darkness, under the gallery, past the sarcophagi of Vasco da Gama and Camões, before you reach the great nave of the church. The effect is like pushing through the undergrowth into a spacious forest of palm trees: trunk-like columns of different widths, encrusted with decoration, gently rise to meet the vaulting ribs which seem to grow out of them like leaves or branches. This one of the most exhilarating interiors in the whole of Portugal. The Renaissance capela-mór or chancel, built fifty years later, looks inhibited by comparison.

If anything, the cloisters are even more beautiful: two vaulted storeys, the arches of each bay sub-divided into two more arches and once again a profusion of decorative detail: Renaissance medallions and friezes combined with more characteristically Manueline ropes, twisted coral and spiralling columns. The longer neo-Manueline extension to the west of the monastery is nineteenth-century and houses the **Archeological Museum** with the **Maritime Museum** at the far end.

Heading westward along the Rua de Belém (the high street to the west of the monastery), you have the choice of several good restaurants, but from Nos. 88–94, there is a unique *pastelaria*, not to be missed, the **Fabrica de Pasteis de Belém**. The pastry-shop makes and sells a local variant of the popular *pastel de nata*, usually a rather ordinary custard tart, which is here somehow transformed into one of the gastronomic wonders of Lisbon. The place does not seem to have changed much since it was established over a hundred years ago; carved cabinets and drawers line the shop area and *azulejos* decorate the rest of it. White-jacketed and slightly grumpy waiters bring your pastries with shakers of cinnamon and sugar.

Further along the same street is the eighteenth-century **Palácio de Belém**, once a royal palace, today the official residence of the President of the Republic. A museum of coaches now stands in the palace's former riding school.

Return along the Tagus into the centre of Lisbon.

Outra Banda

2 days/175km/from Lisbon

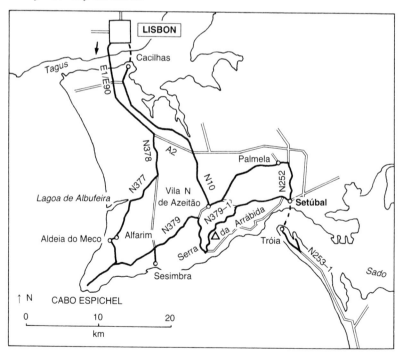

The peninsula south of Lisbon formed between the river Tagus and the river Sado is known as the *Outra Banda* (other side) though it is still a part of Estremadura. Apart from a motorway, it has changed little since George

Borrow travelled through it in 1835, distributing bibles and worrying about bandits, on his way to Spain: 'We reached a sandy plain studded with stunted pine; the road was little more than a footpath, and as we proceeded, the trees thickened and became a wood.' It is still sandy, full of pines and a little bleak but with some splendid moments, such as the jagged promontory at Cabo Espichel and the warm and sheltered beaches along its southern side.

Head south from **LISBON** (see p. 15) via the **Ponte 25 de Abril**, the longest suspension bridge in Europe. Its name commemorates the 1974 Revolution, although it was originally called after Salazar when it opened in 1966. This

The pilgrim church and lodgings at Cabo Espichel

approach to the *Outra Banda*, does not look promising. The vast and ugly monument of Christ the King gazes down on miles of necessary, but badly planned, suburban sprawl. Stay on the motorway and you sweep through it quickly enough. Soon after leaving this road for the N378 you start to pass through the small pine woods for which the region is well known. Shortly after the village of Fernão Ferro, turn right onto the N377 which takes you to the **Lagoa De Albufeira**, a long sandy lagoon surrounded by trees, popular with wind surfers and a suitable stopping point for a picnic. There is also a camp site here.

Continue south along the same road and after 6km you reach Alfarim, where you leave the N377, turning right for the **Aldeia do Meco**, a cliff-top village close to a fine stretch of good beaches. From here take any of the small roads south and before long you reach the N379, at which point you turn right for **CABO ESPICHEL**. This is another promontory jutting dramatically into the Atlantic but made rather more mysterious than those of Cabo de Roca or Cabo Raso by its rugged coastline and the abandoned church and pilgrim houses perched at its edge. The road simply stops here by a stone cross at the opening of a square, lined on opposite sides by semi-derelict two-storey houses built over an arcade, at the head of which stands an equally decrepit eighteenth-century church.

When we visited, on a rainy afternoon in November, there was nobody around except a shepherd and his flock and an old lady listening to a radio. At one point, on the headland beyond the church, sunlight suddenly pierced the storm clouds, forming a circle of light on the water, and it was possible to comprehend the strange legend of the Virgin Mary appearing out of the sea riding on a mule. Marks up the cliff side near the Lagosteiros beach, once believed to have been the mule's hoof prints, are now thought to have been left by dinosaurs. Since the fifteenth century there has been a shrine here, popular with sailors who, when they sighted it, knew that they were almost home. In summer, the supernatural atmosphere evaporates somewhat as carloads of day trippers arrive and a bar suddenly materialises at the top of the square.

A short walk away, across cliff tops thick with wild thyme, stands the lighthouse, which we were shown round by an immensely house-proud keeper. The complex crystal and brass mechanism—spotlessly clean—of the light itself was manufactured at the turn of the century in Paris and reassembled here. Unlike the church, it is still in use, this coastline being notoriously perilous for shipping.

From Cabo Espichel, retrace your route a short way along N379, through quite barren windswept terrain. After about 5km, you reach the **Estalagem dos Zimbros** on your left and after another 6km you come to the crossroads at Santana, from where you can either continue straight or make a small detour to **SESIMBRA**. This was, until quite recently, a small fishing village but is now a very popular and overcrowded resort complete with camp site. The castle between Santana and Sesimbra, whose foundations are Moorish, was actually built to consolidate the Christian reconquest of the south and was given by Dom Sancho II in 1236 to the Order of Santiago, who already controlled the nearby castle at Palmela. If you wish to avoid Sesimbra but need some lunch, there is a good restaurant, the **Angelus** (223 1340), at Santana.

Rejoining or continuing along the N379 north-eastwards takes you, after about 5km, past the entrance to the seventeenth-century Calhariz Palace (owned by the Duke of Palmela but not, unfortunately, open to the public) and, after a further 4km, you turn right for the **Serra da Arrábida**. After a while, when the road divides, follow the left-hand fork (the N379–1, the upper road to Setúbal), which will take you into the heart of the *serra*. This is now an official **Nature Park** and if you visit here in springtime, preferably in early May, it is alive with a wide range of Mediterranean flowers. Later in the year, some may find it a little too hot and dry to make use of the many footpaths provided for walkers. Not far along this road you can see on your right the **Franciscan Convent of Arrábida**, founded in 1542 in what was then a very isolated and desolate spot (see p. 17).

This road eventually joins the lower road near the mouth of the River Sado with the Tróia peninsula visible over to your right. **SETÚBAL**, just a few kilometres along the river from here, is a likeable town which has managed to preserve its old centre in the face of substantial industrial development. Salt has been extracted from the estuary since Roman times, and it still is an important fishing centre. The town gives its name to a popular dessert wine made from muscatel grapes and is also famous as the birthplace of the Romantic poet, Bocage, whose face is seen on old 200$ notes and on a popular brand of coffee. The Manueline style of architecture has one of its earliest expressions here in the Igreja de Jesus, a small church whose nave is supported by six unusual columns, made up of three strands of stone seemingly twisted around each other; the ribbing in the apse is similarly twisted like rope. This is the work of Diogo Boitac, the first master of works at the Jerónimos Monastery in Belém, and dates from the 1490s. The adjacent museum, housed in the former Monastery of Jesus, contains a fine sequence of paintings by the sixteenth-century Master of Setúbal.

The peninsula of **TRÓIA** is reached by taking a ferry-boat at Setúbal; they leave every 30 minutes and take about twenty minutes to reach the outer bank of the Sado. In spite of some ugly tourism-related development, it is still worth a visit for the ruins, as well as for the many different species of birds that may be seen there. When you leave the ferry, the road stretching ahead leads eventually to the village of Comporta but after about 2km you see a sign indicating horse-riding to your left. This is a way to the Roman ruins: drive along a sand track, past the riding school and a couple of kilometres on you come to a large yard with a chapel up on the right and a large derelict house. The ruins are on your right, and are open from 9am to 5pm.

These ruins date back to the first century BC and there is great controversy as to whether they are the ruins of the Roman town of Cetobriga or whether these are in Setúbal. The latter seems to be more likely, as Briga means hill or mount in Celtic and Setúbal stands at the base of a hill, whereas Tróia is absolutely flat. Tróia seems to have been mainly the industrial area of a larger town—a great quantity of fish-salting tanks were found here, which were used to produce *garum*, a paste made out of fish and other seafood.

The excavation of the residential area was first ordered by Dona Maria I and, although much is still buried under the sand, you can see some ruins of what apparently were the Baths and also some public rooms. The large number of fish-salting tanks, rectangular in shape, with rounded corners, were later used, towards the end of the Roman Empire, as tombs, and Tróia continued to be used as a cemetery until the late Middle Ages. Besides being an industrial area and an ideal funeral ground, it was also a religious centre; first pagan and then early Christian.

From here, if you do not want to return to Lisbon, you are ideally situated for the journey south, either via Alcácer do Sal, 30km to the east, or along N261 which follows the coast.

Retrace your route back to Setúbal but then leave the town on the road marked for **PALMELA**, a mere 5km to the north. This little town is completely dominated by its substantial castle, which contains the **Pousada Palmela** (235 1226) and provides wonderful views of the hills to the west and Lisbon to the north. Dom Afonso Henriques captured

Palmela for the second time in 1166 but it was devastated in 1191 by Yussuf, Caliph of Morocco, as part of his successful campaign to recapture Silves. As a result, it was rebuilt and occupied by the Order of Santiago, who later made a significant contribution to the Christian reconquest of the south.

After leaving Palmela, take the road (once again the N379) which will eventually lead you to Vila Nogueira de Azeitão. Passing three windmills to your left, you enter countryside rich with vines, the area round Setúbal being one of the few demarcated regions south of the Tagus. Just outside the village of Quinta do Anjo turn left, and when you get to the main road (N10) turn right and not long after you reach the **Quinta da Bacalhôa**, the most beautiful house in this region. It is easy to miss the entrance gate on your right as the house is hidden by hedges and, anyway, not easily accessible to the public, since it is privately owned, though polite enthusiasm will probably gain you entrance. If successful, you will see an Italianate palace (possibly by Sansovino) built at the end of the fifteenth century on an L-shaped plan, with three circular towers and some wonderfully simple Renaissance arcades. By the 1930s it had fallen into disrepair, but was then carefully restored by its American owner, Mrs Scoville, whose family still own it. (In fact, it is possible, at considerable cost, to book the Quinta on a weekly basis by writing to Thomas Scoville, 3637 Veazey Street, Washington, D.C. 2008, USA.)

A little less expensive, similarly Italianate and almost as beautiful, is the **Quinta das Torres**, a few kilometres along the road (but again not visible from it) at **VILA FRESCA DE AZEITÃO**. Built about a hundred years later than Bacalhôa, it has a charmingly geometrical façade with a Venetian entrance and two small towers at each end, topped by pyramids. Access is not a problem here, since it is now an Estalagem (208 0001) with a good restaurant, the perfect place to try some of the local wines.

The entrance to the Quinta dos Torres is on the left, as you come from Bacalhôa, almost opposite the winery of one of the biggest manufacturers in the area, J.M. da Fonseca. This firm makes some very good red wines; Periquita, a full fruity red being particularly well thought of, as is the wine from the Bacalhôa estate made by João Pires.

From here, it is only a few kilometres to **VILA NOGUEIRA DE AZEITÃO**, a small, pretty town with some fine houses, including the rather austere Palace of the Dukes of Aveiro, and the church of São Lourenço, which contains some good *azulejos*. On the first Sunday of each month there is a busy market selling country fare including a local cheese, *queijo fresco*, made from ewe's milk.

To return to Lisbon, keep to the N10 and after about 9km cross the motorway, before passing through numerous nondescript suburbs, Corroios, Laranjeiro, and Cova da Piedade. At the latter, turn off if you want to return via the bridge, but if you continue, you will eventually reach **CACILHAS**, where a car ferry runs every twenty minutes to Cais de Sodré in central Lisbon. This crossing is worth taking in almost any weather for the perspective it gives of the city's width and hilliness, and for the play of light on the water and the soft whiteness of the buildings.

Alcobaça and Batalha

2–3 days/190km/from Alcobaça to the Berlengas

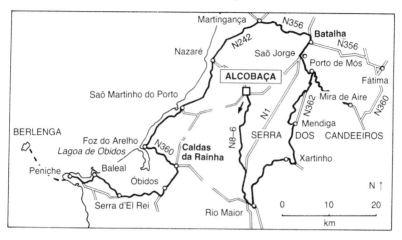

Two great medieval abbeys, at Alcobaça and Batalha, celebrate respectively the extension of the kingdom into Moorish territory and the securing of the kingdom against the threat of Spain. This is where the route begins before heading towards the coast to visit two important centres of the fishing industry, Nazaré and Peniche. The first preserves many traditional customs and costumes, while the second is rather more modern.

In 1153, in gratitude to God for his victory at Santarém six years before, Afonso Henriques founded and endowed the great **Abbey of Santa Maria** at **ALCOBAÇA**. The abbey was to be a Cistercian one, in acknowledgement of the help given by the Order's dominant figure, Abbot Bernard of Clairvaux, in winning papal recognition for the Kingdom of Portugal. The Cistercian order was particularly devoted to a life of simplicity and hard work and, since its arrival in Portugal in *c.*1139, had done much to recultivate lands abandoned as a result of the Christian/Moorish conflict. The site of the abbey, where the rivers Alcoa and Baça meet, was extremely fertile and the region is still a major fruit-growing area.

The church is entered through the remodelled Baroque façade of 1723 (the portal and the rose window are of the original Gothic). The impression inside the nave is of brightness and great depth, with a feeling of spaciousness increased by the unusual inner shafts which terminate three-quarters of the way down the piers. This architectural grandeur and simplicity is typically Cistercian, but has been revealed today only by the wholesale removal of the church's non-medieval additions, notably the eighteenth-century decorative work of Willian Elsden.

The church contains many beautiful things: the chapel with the tombs of Dom Afonso II and Dom Afonso III; the Manueline doorway into the sacristy and, most famously, the tombs of Dom Pedro I and the legendary Inês de Castro in the transepts. Their story (told in Canto III of Camões's The Lusiads (see the Bibliography)) is one of the most celebrated and romantic in Portuguese history. Before Pedro became king, he fell in love with a Galician noblewoman, Inês de Castro, a cousin of his Spanish wife, Constanza. When Constanza died, Inês openly lived with Pedro and bore him two sons. Inês's brothers had political ambitions, and several Portuguese nobles, fearing this foreign influence on their future king, intrigued against her. Claiming the support of Pedro's father, Dom Afonso IV, they murdered her. Pedro then rose up against his father but was eventually pacified. On his accession, in 1357, he had the murderers bloodily executed, declared Inês to have been his wife and made his court pay homage to her body, exhumed and seated on a throne next to his. Today their tombs lie foot to foot, hers in the north transept, his in the south. Though badly vandalised by French soldiers in 1811, they remain two of the finest surviving examples of Portuguese Gothic carving.

To the north of the church is the early fourteenth-century Cloister of Dom Dinis, leading to the Chapter House, which contains several fine Baroque terracotta statues of angels and saints, originally in the transept chapels. Also off the cloister is '. . . the most magnificent kitchen that ever priestly luxury defines; a brook flowing through it to supply water and wash the dishes, and an opening into the refectory, that dishes may not cool on their way' (Southey). The whole kitchen, including the vast

The tomb of Inês de Castro

central chimney, is covered in pale blue tiles dated 1725. The refectory itself has an arcaded flight of steps, set into the wall, at the top of which is a platform where suitable texts would have been read during meals. Still on the same floor, the Sala dos Reis is so called for its collection of near identical statues of all the Portuguese kings up to Dom José I. It also contains azulejos depicting the foundation of the monastery and its early history. Off the cloister's upper storey (added in the early sixteenth century) is the enormous thirteenth-century dorter or dormitory. The rest of the building is mostly of a later date and is now used for various municipal purposes.

The abbey was one of the richest and most powerful in the country, its loyalty having being rewarded in grants and land by successive Portuguese kings but, by the time of its closure in 1834, its corruption and decline was total. The town, still dominated both physically and historically by the abbey, is a pleasant place to stay and a good base for touring the surrounding area. The **Tourist Office** is opposite the church and there is a good restaurant, the **Celeiro dos Frades**, just off the upper side of the Praça Dom Afonso Henriques (to the left of the Abbey).

Leaving the town by the N8–6 for Rio Maior, head south through the villages of Évora de Alcobaça, Turquel and Benedita until you join the motorway (N1). Continuing south for about 2km, you reach a junction where you take the left-hand turning marked to Alto da Serra. After another 1km, you pass through the aptly named village of Salinas, with its salt mine, before turning left for Alcobertas. The mountain range, the **Serra dos Candeeiros**, visible since leaving Alcobaça, now lies ahead. This range is not high but very dry and stony, with virtually no trees or vegetation on its slopes. Farmers use the limestone for making divisions of the land and these walls make odd patterns like ringworm scars on the barren hillside. The valleys through which you drive are, however, extremely fertile and olive groves abound. The village houses are mainly long, one-storey buildings, usually white, sometimes trimmed with blue or ochre. They are similar to the houses of the Alentejo region but they tend to be detached rather than terraced, and they lack the large, ornate chimneys of the south.

After passing through the village of Xartinho, turn left at the junction with the N362. At Mendiga turn left again for a scenic detour, rejoining the N362 just south of **Porto de Mós**. Perhaps the green pinnacles of the castle here, recently added to two of its five towers, create too much of a fairy-tale effect but it had become an unusually palatial and comfortable fortress at the hands of the Count of Ourém. It had been in his family only since 1385, when it was awarded to his grandfather, the great Portuguese general, Nuno Álvares Pereira, following his victory at the Battle of Aljubarrota (see p. 32). In fact, the Portuguese army stopped here two days before the battle, en route from Abrantes via Tomar.

A short (circular) detour east will take you, after about 13km to **MIRA DE AIRE**, the site of subterranean caves discovered in 1947 and now open to the public. A forty-minute guided tour takes you through the fantastically weird formations of limestone and other minerals, down (over 100m) to an underwater lake. It is all dramatically lit to maximise the other-worldliness of the experience. There are other caves in the area at Santo António and São Mamede. Also nearby is the shrine of **FÁTIMA** (see Introduction) recommended only to devout Catholics or religious voyeurs. Unless you wish to visit Fátima, return to Porto do Mós via the village of Bouçeiros.

About 5km north west of Porto do Mós, just before regaining the motorway, you reach **SÃO JORGE**, the actual site of the important Battle of Aljubarrota, the climax of an intense and bitter dynastic struggle. Following the death of Dom Fernando (a son of Pedro I) in 1383, his wife, Leonor Teles, a Spaniard with a Spanish lover, became regent. Her daughter Beatriz, probably fathered by Fernando but married to King Juan of Castile, was the recognised heir to the throne. Her claim, however, was contested by João, the bastard son of Pedro I and Grand Master of the military order of Avis. Although most of the nobility supported Beatriz, popular and mercantile support was for João of Avis and, in April 1385, he was appointed King, João I, by the Cortes at Coimbra. On 14 December of the same year (with the help of about 500 English archers) his army defeated a larger Castilian force at the Battle of Aljubarrota.

On the site where Nuno Álvares Pereira (João's great general and advisor) issued his orders, there now stands the small chapel of São Jorge, where visiting travellers can drink from a jug of fresh water that has been provided daily for this purpose since the battle. Nearby, as well as a small military museum, there is a frieze commemorating the victory and beside the church stand simple blocks of stone representing foot soldiers and bowmen. But the real monument of the victory is the Dominican monastery of **Santa Maria da Vitória** at **BATALHA** (Battle), just 4km along the motorway to the north east. Unfortunately, the road passes damagingly close to the west front of the building, begun in 1388. It is likely that English masons helped work on the building—some of the detailing recalls the English perpendicular style, while the window tracery seems more French.

Inside, the nave of the church appears immensely high but, in order to achieve this, the piers are of a thickness that is slightly oppressive, especially after the spaciousness of Alcobaça. Immediately to the right, as you enter, is the Founder's Chapel (c.1430), surmounted by an octagonal lantern with a stellar vault. It contains, beneath the lantern, the tombs of Dom João I and his English Queen, Philippa of Lancaster, and, along the south side, the tombs of four of their sons: Fernando, João, Henriques (known as 'the Navigator') and Pedro. There are two cloisters: the Royal Cloister with its extraordinary arches, half-filled with a delicate Manueline 'screen' of exotic tracery and, next to it, the simpler Cloister of Dom Afonso V.

The tomb of Portugal's unknown soldier has been placed in the Chapter House, whose daringly ambitious vault spans some 19m. But the oddest, and perhaps the most beautiful, part of the building is the Capelas Imperfeitas (Unfinished Chapels), intended as a Royal Mausoleum and built on to the east end of the church by order of Dom Duarte, who succeeded Dom João I. Like the Royal Cloister, it was extravagantly transformed by Dom Manuel I, whose Master of Works, Mateus Fernandes, is responsible for the vast trefoil-arched portal. This is smothered in decorative detail, more vegetal than nautical, which includes snails and artichokes, as well as the repetition of Dom Duarte's motto 'leauté faray tam yasaray' (I will always be loyal). Greater things were planned but, after the completion of the gallery above the chapels in 1533, Dom João III diverted the skilled labour to other projects in Belém and Tomar, leaving the great stumps of the half-built composite piers (which were to support another vaulted octagon) stranded and abandoned to the elements.

The town itself is disappointing, although a few old houses still remain and, even after the splendours of the Capelas Imperfeitas, the Manueline portal of the church is worth seeking out. But the indignity of the nearby motorway and the drab new complex of tourist shops, jarringly close to the abbey, makes the place seem, at worst, like a glorified service station.

Rejoin the motorway and continue north a short distance before turning left onto the N356, then, at Martingança, bear left along the N242 for Nazaré. Just before arriving at Nazaré, turn off for the lesser known upper district of **SÍTIO**. Here, in 1182, the *alcaide* of Porto de Mós, Dom Fuas Roupinho, built a chapel to the Virgin in gratitude for a miraculous escape. One foggy morning, while out hunting, he was lured to the edge of the cliffs by 'the devil in the guise of a stag'. Rider and horse were prevented from tumbling to their deaths only by a last-minute prayer to Our Lady of Nazaré. Locals, if pressed, will argue as to which unconvincing mark on the precipice is actually the hoofprint of the *alcaide*'s horse.

In fact, **NAZARÉ** (Nazareth) derives its name from a fourth-century image of the Virgin, originally from the Holy Land, deposited here for safekeeping by Dom Rodrigo, the last Visigoth King. The image was lost when he died but was found by shepherds some 400 years later. The site became an important place of pilgrimage and is still attended by *círios*, organised festive processions, with children dressed as angels, from a neighbouring parish. These take place between 5 August and 15 September. The twin-towered seventeenth-century church replaced one that was built for Dom Fernando in 1370.

The main town, down by the beach, may be reached by funicular and is much more modern, although the inhabitants of this stretch of coast are rather fancifully believed to be connected to the original Phoenician settlers on account of their grey-blue eyes. Today they are fisherman, famous for their costume and for their boats. A variety of brightly coloured plaids is used for the men's shirts, as well as for the women's skirts (usually worn over seven petticoats). On their heads, the men wear long woollen stocking caps and the women wear strange pill-box hats (with a pom-pom on one side) that, supposedly, help to balance the large baskets of fish that

A meia-lua *fishing boat at Nazaré*

they carry up from the shore. The local boats are even more curious. There are two principal types: the *meia-lua* (half-moon)—named after its high, crescent-shaped prow—has very long oars and a crew of six or seven; and the *bateira de mar*, which is smaller, flatter-bottomed and with a crew of only three. Both, but particularly the *meia-lua*, are brightly coloured and highly decorated with symbols (saints, crosses, eyes) painted onto their prows. In the old days, because of the lack of a jetty, the larger boats were pushed out to sea by gangs of men and hauled in by oxen but since 1985, when a harbour wall was built, this is rarely seen.

Despite being the most famous and popular fishing village in the country, Nazaré has kept its charm and some of its customs intact but it is probably a place to be avoided at the height of the summer. The **Tourist Office** is on the seafront and there is no shortage of accommodation.

Continue southwards, following the coast but not always in sight of it, until you reach **SÃO MARTINHO DO PORTO**. This increasingly popular village possesses a fine sheltered beach along its bay—though it looked a little grubby the day we visited it. There is a substantial amount of new building going on but it is not recommended as a place to stay. The N242 heads inland here, but follow the small, coastal road past the great sand dune by Salir do Porto. Along this road, reeds have been planted to act as a windbreak. At Foz de Arelho, the coast road is stopped, as is the coastline itself, by the Lagoa de Óbidos, a large salt-water lagoon, famed for its eels.

At this point, head inland along the N360 for the spa town of **CALDAS DA RAINHA**, known for its sulphur springs and for Queen Leonor, the wife of Dom João III, who founded a hospital here in 1485. Her statue faces the park, in the centre of which is a museum dedicated to and housing works by José Malhoa (and other late nineteenth-century Portuguese painters). Caldas contains two other museums, both near the park: a contemporary sculpture museum founded by the sculptor, Antonio Duarte, and the Ceramics Museum, which includes examples of the local, highly naturalistic green-ware by the famous *fin-de-siècle* sculptor and potter, Rafael Bordalo Pinheiro. Apart from these attractions, Caldas is not an especially interesting town, although the hospital church of Nossa Senhora do Populo, with its Manueline bell-tower and chancel, is worth visiting.

More interesting, and only 6km to the south on the N8, is the beautiful walled hill-town of **ÓBIDOS**, which you reach by turning off the road soon after passing the enormous, hexagonal Baroque church of Senhor da Pedra. It is possible to walk right round the town along the restored battlements (cars may be left in front of the castle, which now houses the pousada) but the charm of the place lies in its narrow cobbled streets; its brilliant white houses trimmed with blue or ochre and hung with flowers; and the small, perfectly proportioned *largo* that almost disguises the hill on which it is set. Above this *largo*, on the main street (the Rua Direita), stands a *pelourinho* marked with a fishing net and a crown. Queen Leonor spent several years here in mourning for her only son and the heir to the throne, Dom Afonso, who was crushed to death after falling from his horse when out hunting with a friend. His body was carried to a nearby cottage in a fishing net and the Queen then adopted the net as her emblem. Until 1832, the town was entitled Casas das Rainhas (Houses of the Queens), on account of this and because of its association with other Portuguese queens: it had been a wedding present to the Holy Queen Isabel from her husband, Dom Dinis, and in the sixteenth century, Catherine of Austria, Dom João III's wife, built the aqueduct which still stands, running southwards from the town.

The church of Santa Maria, standing to the east of the largo, has a Renaissance portal with a statue of the Virgin and, inside, on the north wall, the tomb of João de Noronha (the *alcaide-mor* for the town). In a chapel, to the right of the high altar, is an outstanding example of the work of Josefa d'Ayala (or Josefa de Óbidos), a local artist working in the seventeenth century. The altar-piece depicts episodes from the life of St Catherine. At the top is the central panel of 'The Mystic Marriage' (her spiritual betrothal to Christ), with smaller panels of St Teresa and St Francis on either side. Below is 'St. Catherine disputing with the Philosophers' (who were sent to convert her by the Emperor) and, on the right, 'The Destruction of the Wheel' (on which she was to be tortured). More of Josefa's work can be seen in the town's small museum nearby.

During the summer, Óbidos comes to life at night and is full of people who stroll up and down the narrow streets or pop in and out of the numerous bars to drink the local *ginginha* (a kind of cherry brandy) or the famous *toupeiro*, a very sweet liqueur, the ingredients of which are a well-kept secret.

Much of the land between here and the coastline has been reclaimed, over the centuries, from the sea. At one point, boats could reach Óbidos and at the time of Afonso Henriques, Peniche was still an island. This has made the land a flat and fertile plain: what the Portuguese call a *veiga*.

After leaving Óbidos, continue southwards for a short while before turning right onto the N114 to Peniche. **Serra D'el Rei** contains the ruins of a palace built for Dom Pedro I, and good views of Peniche. Here you turn right for Ferrel and **Beleal**. The latter is still, practically, an island connected to the mainland by a thin strip of land, worth crossing, when the tide is out, for its views of the sea and the distant Berlengas Islands.

From here, continue along the coast road until you regain the main road and, after a few kilometres, reach **PENICHE**. The name suggests another Phoenician connection, or perhaps it is a corruption of the Latin word for peninsula—nobody is quite sure. Like Beleal, it used to be an island but now a long, thin isthmus, lined with some good, sandy beaches, connects it to the mainland. Regular attacks by pirates led to the *forteleza*, or fortress, being built in 1557. Twelve years later, when the country was united with Spain, it managed to withhold an attack by Sir Francis Drake and several thousand English troops attempting to reinstate the pretender to the Portuguese throne, Dom António, Prior of Crato. Trade links with Flanders are suggested by the intricate lacework—*Rendas de Bilros*—made here. Strings are knotted by hand, using a small, pear-shaped bobbin, to create the complex patterns. Examples may be seen at the museum and may be purchased in the town.

Today, Peniche is an important centre for the fishing industry: sardine and tuna are caught and canned here in great numbers and the feeling is of a busy working town, rather than a tourist attraction. Of course it abounds in fish restaurants, the **Restaurant Meiavia** near the market, being particularly good. And there are things to see: the fortress, now a museum of local history and archeology was, during the Salazar years, one of the most notorious prisons controlled by PIDE (the secret police). From here, in 1960, the imprisoned communist leader, Alvaro Cunhal, made a daring escape from his cell to a waiting boat. Nearby, the Sanctuary of Nossa Senhora dos Remédios contains some outstanding Baroque azulejos: *trompe l'œil* putti and caryatids from scenes from the life of the Virgin

Mary. These were designed by António de Oliveira Bernardes but carried out by his son, Policarpo. From outside the chapel, you can see what for many is the main reason for coming to Peniche, the **BERLENGAS ISLANDS**.

Of the group of islands, only the main one, **Berlenga Grande**, can be visited. Boats from Peniche harbour run twice a day during June and September (10am and 5pm) and three times a day during July and August. The boat trip takes about an hour and is not recommended for those who suffer from seasickness. It is possible to stay on the island: there is a camp site, which can get very busy, and a pensão in the offshore **Forte de São João Baptista**, which is linked to the island by bridge and was once the home of Jeronymite monks. Apart from caves to explore and a footpath right round the island, there is little to do here. Its greatest functional value today is as a stopping-off point for migratory birds.

2 THE RIBATEJO

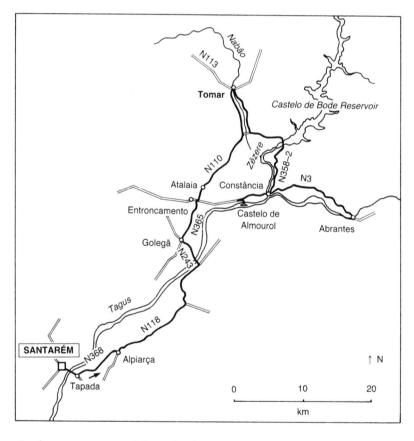

As the name suggests (*riba* = bank; *Tejo* = Tagus) this region lies in the valley of the Tagus river whose alluvial soil makes this a highly fertile area, intensively farmed in many areas. The plains beside the river, known as the *lezíria*, are ideal for the growing of grain, particularly rice, since they are heavily flooded at the beginning of each year. Beyond the plains to the north, around Tomar, smallholders cultivate fruit and olives, whereas on the southern banks of the river (closer to the Alentejo) the growing of eucalyptus and cork oak trees is more common. For the Portuguese, the Ribatejo is synonymous with the breeding of horses and bulls, primarily for fighting. There are several stud farms in the region, including the national one, the Estação Zootécnica Nacional, near Santarém. On the plains where they graze, the bulls and horses are tended by mounted *campinos* who control the herd by means of long wooden poles, carried like a lance and used for prodding the animals into line. The men traditionally wear green stocking-caps, black knee breeches and a red waistcoat. Every year in early July there is a festival at Vila Franca de Xira called Colete Encarnado (red waistcoat) where the *campinos* show off their skills in bull-herding displays and there is bull-fighting and bull-running in the streets.

The Ribatejo

2–3 days/115km/from Santarém to Abrantes

The Tagus (or Tejo) is a vast river stretching from beyond the Spanish border, almost all the way across the peninsula. This route follows its course upstream from Santarém (the furthest that Almeida Garrett got in his *Travels in my Homeland*) along the flooded pastureland to the beginning of one of its main tributaries, the Zêzere river. The highlight of the route is Tomar; only a small country town but possessing in the Convento de Cristo the finest complex of buildings in the country.

SANTARÉM, once an important fortress town, now an agricultural centre, is the capital of the Ribatejo region. The Romans called it Scallabis but its present name is derived from the cult of Santa Iria, a nun martyred at Tomar in 653AD, whose body (or coffin) floated down three rivers before coming to rest here. A statue found in the river and thought to represent the saint now stands at the water's edge. The city's eventual recapture from the Moors was achieved in 1147 by Dom Afonso Henriques with the help of the Knights Templar.

The main square, Praça de Sá da Bandeira, is where the murderers of Inês de Castro were tortured and executed by Pedro I (see p. 30). On its southern side is the handsome but austere Seminary church built for the Jesuits in the 1680s. Generally the town's monuments have suffered over the centuries: little remains of the castle, the Alcáçova, but heading south-eastwards through the town towards the Portas do Sol (Gates of the Sun) you will pass the sixteenth-century Marvila church which has a fine Manueline door and chancel arch. The church's outstanding feature, however, is the blue-and-white, floor-to-ceiling geometrical *azulejos*, installed in 1617. Just to its south is another church, the fifteenth-century Nossa Senhora de Graça whose façade, with its beautiful rose window, is reminiscent of the Abbey of Alcobaça. The church contains the tomb of the navigator, Pedro Álvares Cabral, who reached Brazil in 1500, as well as monuments to various members of the Meneses family including Pedro de Meneses, the first governor of Ceuta. In the nearby church (now a museum) of São João Alparão is the tooth of Duarte de Meneses, housed in an ornate gothic tomb, this being all that was left of him following his death in Africa in 1464.

A short walk takes you to the gardens of the Portas do Sol, and what remains of the old Moorish citadel. The broad views of the Tagus and the flat plains of the Ribatejo stretching out before you give a good idea of why the city was considered impregnable.

The lush plains are the grazing land of bulls and horses bred up for the *tourada*, or bull-fight, and watched over by the *campinos*, the Ribatejan cowboys. The bull-fights are exclusive to the south, particularly the Ribatejo, and contain all the ritual, costume and cruelty of their Spanish counterparts but with the emphasis placed on skilled horsemanship. The *cavaleiro*, dressed in a stylised eighteenth-century costume and mounted on a Lusitanian stallion, lures the bull towards him into a position where he can place his short spears or *bandarillas*, into the animal's neck. Having achieved this with six successive spears displaying the maximum amount of arrogant poise in teasing and frustrating the bull, the *cavaleiro* leaves the ring to be replaced by the *forçados*. These are a team of eight men, on foot, who form a line in front of the bull and when it charges, pile into it in an attempt to bring it to a standstill. The leader clings to its head while one of the others attaches himself to the bull's tail. This looks as idiotic as it sounds and the claim that the Portuguese bull-fight is less cruel than the Spanish just because the animal is not killed in the ring, is sentimental and disingenuous since clearly the bull is not led from the arena to a happy retirement or to convalesce. For those who find the prospect irresistible, **VILA FRANCA DE XIRA** (about 30km from Lisbon and 46km from Santarém) is the acknowledged centre for the 'sport'. It can also be seen at the many fairs held in Santarém, among which is the Milagre Fair (from the second Sunday in April), the great Ribatejo Fair (from the fourth Sunday in May) and the Piedade Fair (from the second Sunday in October).

After crossing the Tagus, turn left at Tapada onto the N368. Ten km further east in the direction of the river is the small town of **ALPIARÇA**. This contains a small museum at the Casa dos Patudos, once the home of the politician, José Relvas, before he left it and his collection to the town. As well as a good collection of Arraiolos carpets, it houses many paintings, including work by Josefa de Óbidos and a portrait of Domenico Scarlatti, briefly court composer to Dom João V. There is a good restaurant, **O Toucinho**, which serves the local speciality, sopa de pedra (stone soup). This was, reputedly, invented by a beggar who persuaded a local cook that his magic stone when added to water would make a delicious soup. So it did, after other ingredients had been added to flavour it.

Continuing along the course of the river, after 21km take the N243 to re-cross to the north bank, just before reaching **GOLEGA**, scene of a famous horse fair every year on 8–11 November. Its parish church has an outstanding Manueline portal with a window above it containing two armillary spheres—the personal emblem of Dom Manuel I. Heading north, on the N365 bypass the town of Entroncamento and at the crossroads on the edge of town, join the N110 which takes you all the way to Tomar. After 2km you reach **ATALAIA**, smaller than Golega but whose equally beautiful church has an ornate Renaissance portal.

After another 19km, through plains made fertile by the river Nabão, you reach the small town of **TOMAR**. As you approach, you see on the hill above the town the great Convent of the Order of Christ, the monument for which the town is most famous. The Knights Templar were established in Tomar as early as 1157. When the order was dissolved worldwide in 1314 on charges of corruption and immorality, the King, Dom Dinis, simply recreated it, naming it the Order of Christ. Its wealth was enormous and from 1417 to 1460, under the Grand Mastership of Prince Henry the Navigator, the order helped to finance the many voyages of exploration and discovery that he initiated.

The heart of the convent is the mysterious *Charola*, the small 16-sided church, based on the Holy Sepulchre in Jerusalem, decorated with paintings and polychromatic sculpture and where the Knights were said to attend mass on horseback. This is entered through the ornate south portal, the work of João de Castilho. Just beyond the *Charola* is the later addition of the choir and, beneath it, the Chapter House. It is the exterior west window of this part of the church, visible from the cloister of Santa Barbara, which displays the most extreme and virtuosic display of Manueline decorative carving, one of the wonders of western architecture. Nautical motifs run riot: the familiar armillary spheres and the cross of the Order of Christ are supported by thick, twisted strands of coral, intricately knotted ropes, floats and flowers and, beneath it all, an old man bearing the roots of a tree on his shoulders. The name of the artist responsible is unknown, although Diogo de Arruda supervised all work here between 1510 and 1514. To reach the window, you must first pass through the two-storey main cloister, built after the conversion of the buildings to a Benedictine establishment. This was begun in 1554 and is the finest expression of Renaissance classicism in Portugal.

Outside the convent, bear left for another slightly earlier Renaissance-style masterpiece, the perfectly proportioned, domed church of Nossa Senhora de Conceição.

This town itself, laid out on a grid plan, is extremely pretty. There is a campsite near the river and several pensions including the **Pensão Nuno Álvares** (049 32873) and the **Pensão Restaurante Luanda** (043 32929). If you are here in an even-numbered year at the beginning of July you should take the opportunity to see the **Festa dos Tabuleiros**, an unusual *romaria*, dedicated to the Holy Spirit. This culminates in a procession of girls dressed in white carrying on their heads dishes piled high with 30 loaves of bread, woven with flowers and with a crown on top. If you miss this, then you may be able to time your visit for the less spectacular Feira de Santa Iria, commemorating the martyr's death (the site is marked by a chapel dedicated to her), held every year on 18–20 October.

The Festa dos Tabuleiros at Tomar

Tomar also contains one of only two synagogues to have survived in Portugal. A square, vaulted structure which seems to date from the fifteenth century, in which case it was in use only for a short while, since the Jews were forcibly converted to Christianity in 1497 (though many continued to practise their religion in secret). It is now the **Abrahão Zacuto Jewish Museum**, containing Hebrew inscriptions and tombstones from all over the country.

Our next destination is **CASTELO DE BODE** to the south east, but before leaving it is worth making a detour north west to look at the remarkable sixteenth-century **Pegoes Aqueduct**. Take the N113, and after a short while an unsurfaced road marked to the left leads you to a valley where the 180 pointed arches carry water to Tomar. For Castelo de Bode, return to Tomar, cross over the river Nabão and head south. After 7km you turn left onto the N385-2 and in a short while reach the **Pousada of São Pedro** (049 38159/38175) close to the great reservoir of Castelo de Bode. This lake supplies Lisbon with both water and electricity and is part of the Zêzere river, a zig-zagging tributary of the Tagus, which has its source high up in the Estrela mountains. You can swim or wind-surf here, or take a boat trip up river through the surrounding pine forests. Though still in the Ribatejo, customs are closer to those of the nearby Beira region and include, at Christmas time, the traditional *matança de porco*, the slaughter and preparation of the pig. The whole family joins in and no part of the animal is discarded, even the blood being used to make the famous *morçelas* sausages—a local speciality.

South of the dam, continue along the N358-2 which leads back to the Tagus and the small town of **CONSTÂNCIA**, called Pugna Tagi by the Romans. It was once an important river port and may have been where the poet Camões was banished, apparently following some romantic indiscretion at the court in Lisbon.

The castle at Almourol

At this point, turn right along the north bank of the Tagus, in order to reach the **Castelo de Almourol**, sign-posted to the left after about 5km. The castle stands on a small island of granite in the middle of the river which you reach by ferry (a man and his rowing boat). The isolated castle is an extremely romantic sight, especially if you see it as we did in the morning mist. Many strange legends are associated with it. One, a sixteenth-century tale, concerns a certain Palmeirim of England, a crusader who, hearing of two princesses guarded by a giant, Almourol, hastens to the castle. When his various chivalric challenges prove unsuccessful, however, he simply decides to continue on his way to the Holy Land; Almourol is eventually overcome by another giant, Dramusiando.

The castle's construction dates back at least as far as Roman times (Roman coins have been found on the site). After being re-captured from the Moors it became part of the lands given over to the Templars, who rebult it in 1171. The founder of the Order in Portugal, Gualdim Pais, is commemorated in an inscription over the castle door. Its inaccessibility has protected it both from attack and from being plundered for building materials after its abandonment. If you visit the castle on St John's Eve, three ghosts are supposed to appear: Dom Ramiro, the last *alcaide*, his daughter, Beatriz, and a young Moorish boy, who avenged the death of his family at the hands of Dom Ramiro by poisoning the *alcaide*'s wife and eloping with his daughter.

After returning to Constância, continue eastwards along the N3 towards the town of **ABRANTES**, which you reach after 16km. Like Santarém, this is a town whose situation on a hill, high above the Tagus, made it defensively important. The castle was enlarged after its recapture from the Moors and it managed to withstand attacks from the *Almohads* in their campaign to win back the area in 1179. It was here that Dom João I and his commander, Nuno Álvares Pereira, quarrelled over whether to face the invading Castilian army or to send a diversionary force to Andalusia. Dom Nuno's wish to fight prevailed and four days later the Battle of Aljubarotta took place (see p. 32). In 1807, the town was captured by the French General Junot, who was rewarded by Napoleon with the title Duke of Abrantes, though within a year, his troops were humiliatingly forced out by the local population.

The town is slightly prettier than Santarém and with no less spectacular views. Between the double walls of the castle, gardens have been planted and nearby the former church of Santa Maria do Castelo houses a museum containing *azulejos* from Seville and sculpture, including tombs of the Almeida family, the Counts of Abrantes. There is a good hotel, the **Hotel de Turismo de Abrantes** (041 21261) and several *pensões*, including the **Pensão Central**. Two culinary specialities are worth trying: *tigeladas*—a sort of sweet omelette, and *palha de Abrantes*—thin, wispy strands of egg, cooked in syrup.

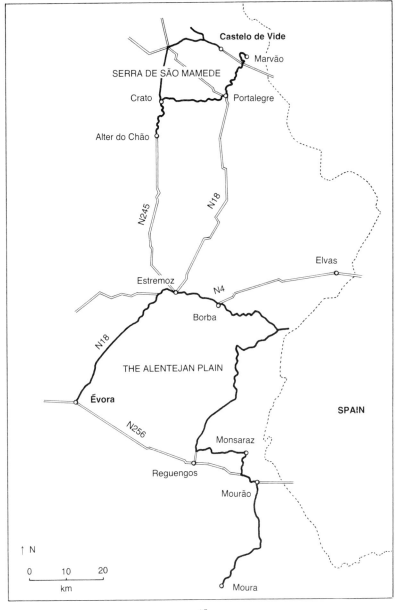

The Alentejo is the largest of all Portugal's provinces, extending south beyond the Tagus river all the way down to the thin strip of coast that is the Algarve. Its vast open plains, though hard and dry, produce most of the country's grain harvest. In late spring this seemingly barren countryside comes alive in a blaze of wild flowers and shrubs. Forests of cork oak break up the plains and have provided Portugal with one of its most prosperous industries since the Middle Ages.

Farming is mostly on huge estates (*latifundios*) and a history of continuous exploitation of the workforce lies behind the longstanding anti-clericism of the region as well as an almost unwavering support for the Communist Party, who still control most of the local councils here. The current government have reversed all the post-revolution agrarian reforms, in many cases returning the land to its original private owners. Currently the Alentejo is suffering from a depression with falling food production and high unemployment.

Many old traditions still survive here. Shepherds can still be seen in their great sheepskin capes and in many areas, especially around Serpa, the highly individual Alentejan choral singing thrives. Unaccompanied, male-voice choirs perform, in simple two- or three-part harmony, passionate songs about the travails and hardships of the land. Another striking characteristic of the province is its almost obsessive cleanliness. It is not just the brilliantly maintained whiteness of individual homes that is striking but also the pristine uniformity within a village or town; often the same colour trim may be found on each house.

The Serra de São Mamede
2 days/100km/from Castelo de Vide

Many guide books suggest that the flatness of the Alentejo makes the landscape monotonous and boring, but this is certainly not true of the following short route which concentrates on three small border towns set in the Alentejo's only real mountain range, the Serra de São Mamede. There is a noticeable contrast in foliage between mountain and plain with the mountains being characterised by a greater variety of trees and shrubs: chestnuts, acacia and willow replace the familiar cork oaks and olive groves of the lowlands.

CASTELO DE VIDE is a small town set in the hills of the Serra de São Mamede, one of the greenest regions of the Alentejo. 'Vide' probably refers to a large, fruitful vine that used to grow where the castle now stands. Those people who still live within the castle walls take great pride in their houses and the streets are full of potted plants and flowers. This is the highest part of the town, with a spectacular view of the tiled roofs of the older quarters, the *solares* and the three-storey houses of the town centre.

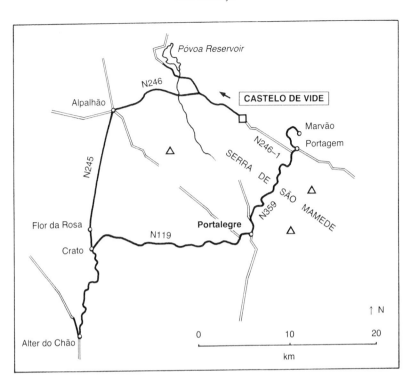

The town was occupied by the Romans in about 50BC and the military road, which ran from their regional capital, Mérida, to the west coast, went through the valley. Dom Dinis rebuilt the ruined Roman-Moorish castle and built the walls of the town, and it was here that he met the ambassadors from the court of Aragon to ratify his marriage to Princess Isabel (later known as the 'Rainha Santa' or Holy Queen, see p. 53).

Taking the street on your left, as you leave the castle, you soon reach the *fonte de vila*, a Renaissance fountain decorated with the Portuguese coat of arms. Castelo de Vide is renowned for mineral waters which are said to relieve diabetes, hypertension and other ailments.

Many of the narrow cobbled streets on the way to the centre of town date from the fourteenth to the sixteenth century and are notable for the variety of their Gothic and Manueline doorways. In one such street a thirteenth-century synagogue was recently discovered. This is in the *Judiaria*, or Jewish quarter, not much different from the rest of town until the fourteenth century when Dom Pedro I had the streets closed off, by means of doors, to restrict the interaction between Christians and Jews. Apparently neither this law, nor another ruling that all Jews must wear a red star, was always strictly enforced and business continued to take place between the two communities through windows cut out of the separating doors, some of which are still visible today.

On the southern descent from the castle, the wider streets contain seventeenth- and eighteenth-century houses, their windows decorated

The fonte de vila *in Castelo de Vide*

with fine wrought-iron work. The Praça de Dom Pedro V, the hub of the town, also contains many fine old buildings: the eighteenth-century Town Hall, the yellow Torre Palace and, opposite this, the great church of Santa Maria. There are several antique and craft shops, and a good restaurant, in the Praça. On summer evenings, women gather in the gardens to crochet together and, if you're lucky, you might hear them singing local songs as they work.

Leaving the town and heading north along the N246, after 7km you reach a junction whose right hand turning leads you to the dam and reservoir of **Povoa**, where you can swim, windsurf and fish. About 10km further west along the N246, lies the small town of **ALPALHÃO**, a typically quiet Alentejan town but one seeming to possess more of the region's enormous chimneys than anywhere else. These chimneys rise, buttress-like, from the ground, on the outside wall of the house. Entering a house normally takes you directly into the kitchen—the most important room—where guests are welcomed and people cook and eat, and often also work. The fireplace stands directly beneath the chimney, making it possible for all the smoke to be absorbed, and so contributing to the impeccable cleanliness that prompts the Portuguese to say that in the Alentejo you can eat off the floor.

Fifteen kilometres south of Alpalhão, along the N245, you reach the village of **FLOR DE ROSA**, the site of a great, fortified monastery, built in 1356 by Álvaro Goncalves Pereira, father of the famous Nuno Álvares Pereira, the 'Holy Constable' (see p. 49). He built it in his capacity as a

Knight of the Order of St John of Jerusalem and, after its completion, assumed the title of Prior of Crato, named after the town, some 2.5km south, which had long been the Order's centre in Portugal. It was the last Prior, Dom António, who persistently but unsuccessfully challenged Philip II of Spain for the Portuguese throne in the 1580s. The remains of the monastery are gradually being excavated and restored after nearly a century of neglect. Crato itself has declined in importance since the seventeenth century but it has some good houses dating from that time.

Continuing south some 15km takes you to **ALTER DO CHÃO**, where it is not unusual to find the use of both granite (a northern building material) and marble (a southern one) within the same building. The beautiful main square, with its wavy-patterned paving, is dominated by the fourteenth-century castle, but also contains a charmingly simple Renaissance fountain and the grandiose, but austere, Solar de Vasconcelos. From here, the **Estação Zootécnica de Alter** is just 3km to the north west. Formerly the royal stud-farm, it was founded by Dom João V in 1748 to supply the royal family with fine mounts. The Alter-Real breed was created here, a variant of the famous Lusitanian horse, and it was one of these horses, 'Gentil', that served as model for the equestrian statue of Dom José I, which stands in the Terreiro do Paço in Lisbon.

After returning to Crato, turn right onto the N119, a straight road leading to **PORTALEGRE**, some 23km to the west. Its old name, Portus Alacer, meant happy place. In fact, its history has not been particularly happy: it includes, for example, two brotherly disputes. In 1299 Dom Dinis besieged his younger brother here, after he refused to recognise his right to the throne and, nearly one hundred years later, Nuno Álvares Pereira defeated his brother, Pedro, who, as *alcaide* of the city and Prior of Crato, had supported the Castilian claim against João of Avis (see p. 32). The first siege took six months and the second twelve hours.

Today, Portalegre is an important centre for cork processing and the Robinson factory, founded by an Englishman in the late nineteenth century, is open to visitors. But the town's real prosperity derives from the development of the textile industry in the sixteenth century and, at the carpet factory, now housed in an old Jesuit convent, every stage of production may be observed. This history of prosperity is reflected in the profusion of grand Baroque houses and mansions (some of the finest in southern Portugal) that may be found in the centre of town, in the Largo de Município and the Praça de Republica and the street that connects them, the Rua do 19 de Junho. One of the grandest, though somewhat dilapidated, is the seventeenth-century Palácio Amarelo (Palace of the Albrancalhas) with its decorative ironwork, outstanding even by the high standards of the region. Nearby, in the Largo do Município, are the Municipal Museum and the cathedral. The former contains archaeological finds, as well as sculptures and ceramics from Roman up to modern times, and includes the memorial stone of Ammaia, the Roman district capital that once existed where Portalegre now stands. On the other side of the street is the Sé, or cathedral, built by the Spanish Bishop of Portalegre in

1556. During the eighteenth century it was greatly restored, hence the Baroque façade with its twin bell-towers. The interior is interesting: with three naves and some good Mannerist paintings in the side altars, an exotically decorated sacristy and an unusual Baroque cloister.

The National Guard now occupy the sixteenth-century Bernardine convent of Nossa Senhora de Conceição, but asking permission at the gate should gain you access. Much of the contents are now housed in the Municipal Museum but the church contains what is thought to be the last masterpiece of Nicolas Chanterène, the tomb of Dom Jorge de Melo, founder of the convent. It is made from Estremoz marble and includes the figures of St Anne and St Joachim (the Virgin's parents), as well as St Bernard and St Benedict and, above, the Assumption of the Virgin surrounded by globe-carrying men, similar to those on the Graça church at Évora.

From Portalegre, the road becomes more twisty as we start to climb higher into the Serra de São Mamede towards the most spectacularly situated of these mountain towns, **MARVÃO**. Cross the N246-1 at Portagem, just before reaching Marvão, you pass by a former convent (now a hospital), founded in 1448 and dedicated to Nossa Senhora da Estrela, the patron saint of Marvão and supposedly its protectress during the many years of war it has endured as a border town. At this point the border, formed by the River Sever, lies a mere 6km away, and the valley is very rich in agricultural soil and minerals. Once again it was Dom Dinis who refortified the town after the conflict with his brother, Afonso. Before that, it had been a Moorish stronghold named after Marvan, the *alcaide* of Coimbra. It fell to the Christians in 1166, although at 862m and with walls seemingly made of the rock itself, it looks impregnable even today.

It's a good idea to leave your car at the entrance of the town and to walk through the narrow cobbled streets or, better still, along the thirteenth-century walls themselves, which are intact almost all the way round. Following the wall will take you to the castle and reveals some very good views, although even better ones can be obtained from the *torre de menagem* in the inner wall of the castle. On a clear day, it is possible to see the Serra da Estrela, 200km to the north. The inner walls also contain the water cistern, which was capable of storing enough water to last the town for six months. While you are looking at the cistern, if you feel brave enough, try singing a few notes. Its amazing acoustics will make any embarrassment worthwhile.

To return to Castelo de Vide, travel via Portagem and the N246-1.

The Alentejan Plain

3–4 days/195km/from Évora to Moura

Hot and dry throughout the summer, this flat part of the country is best visited in early spring (late February) when the many different flowers

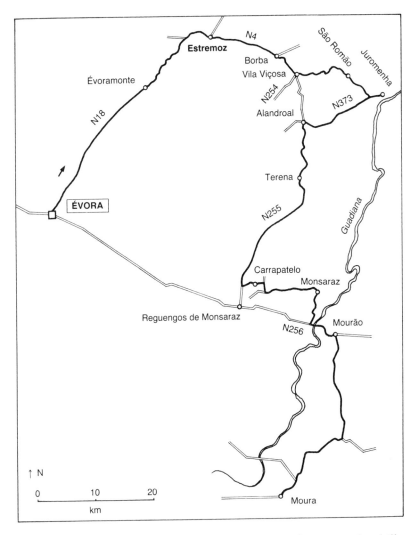

break up the monotony of the plain. Farms are usually set on what hills there are and so are known locally as *Montes*. Human habitation in this region goes back many thousands of years and there is much evidence of megalithic culture, especially around Monsaraz. There is surprisingly little evidence of the Muslim presence which was effectively ended by the military adventurer Geraldo sem Pavor ('without fear') who captured many of the towns on this route at the end of the thirteenth century.

ÉVORA, deep in the heart of the great plains of the Alto Alentejo, is one of the loveliest and best-preserved of all Portuguese towns. Its history goes back at least as far as the Celts, who called it Ebora and made it their southern capital. It contains, at the highest point in the town, the most

51

The Roman temple and the cathedral at Évora

beautiful of the country's Roman remains, the so-called Temple of Diana. Twelve complete columns, with Corinthian capitals of Estremoz marble, have survived. Nearby, other locally-found Roman objects may be seen in the museum, formerly the Archbishop's palace, which also houses a superb collection of sixteenth-century Flemish and Portuguese paintings. Close to this is the great cathedral of Évora, built between 1186 and 1250, the west portal of which is decorated with carvings of the Apostles, probably by local craftsmen. Over the crossing is a tower with a tiled conical roof surrounded by eight smaller turrets. One striking feature of the interior is the oddly emphatic mortaring between the stones—a characteristic shared with the church of São Francisco in the lower part of the town. This church is famous for its morbid Capela dos Ossos (Chapel of Bones), a chapel lined from top to bottom with a neat pattern of skulls and tibia. An inscription near the entrance reads 'Nós ossos que aqui estamos, pelos vossos esperamos' (we bones here are waiting for yours).

The main square of the town is the long Praça do Giraldo with the Renaissance church of Santo Antão at one end. The efficient and friendly **Tourist Office** on the west side of the square will supply you with a map of the town and a list of places to stay. Many of the cheaper places are in the streets west of the Praça. The **Pousada** (066 24051) is behind the Roman Temple and housed in the former **Convento do Loios**, whose ornate cloisters are worth visiting. The **Restaurante Fialho** (066 23079) is one of the best in the region, and quite expensive.

Once outside the city walls, follow the N18, the road to Estremoz. This takes you through flat, open countryside from which, after about 30km, rises the impressively stout and compact castle of **ÉVORAMONTE**, on the western edge of the Serra de Ossa. The small town is contained within the castle walls built by Dom Dinis in 1306, though the central Paço de Homanagem (Palace of the Homage), with its towers tapering like four fat telescopes, is much later. It was built by the Arruda Brothers in 1531 for Dom Jaime, fourth Duke of Bragança. The floor levels are indicated on the exterior by a stone 'girdle' around the building which is knotted above the door. The knot motif is repeated in other Bragança family buildings and refers to their motto 'Depois de Vos, nos' (After you, us), *nos* also being the word for knot. Inside, the magnificent vaulted rooms contain other unusual Manueline motifs such as the flames at the bottom of the thick columns. In 1834, a Convention was signed here at which Dom Miguel finally renounced his claim to the throne, thus ending the War of the Two Brothers (see p. 115).

A mere 17km north east lies the strategically important city of **ESTREMOZ**. Its castle, with a keep almost identical to the one at Beja, dominates the upper town. The palace now houses the luxurious **Pousada da Rainha Santa Isabel** (068 22618) named after the 'Holy Queen' Isabel who died here in 1336 after settling a dispute between her son Afonso IV and Alfonso IX of Castile. Her many charitable acts and the civilising influence she had on her husband Dom Dinis are legendary. One popular story concerns her distributing bread to the poor against the wishes of her husband. When he angrily challenged her to reveal what she was carrying in her apron the bread miraculously turned into roses. The chapel dedicated to her contains *azueljos* depicting scenes from her life.

Next to the pousada entrance is the austere and unfinished facade of the sixteenth-century church of Santa Maria do Castelo and just beyond the church is the magnificent Audience Chamber of Dom Dinis, vaulted and with an arcaded loggia at its front. Over its door is the curious crest of the city, incorporating the national coat of arms flanked by the sun and with a lupin plant below it. The next building to this is the local museum, once a hospital, containing a suite of typically Alentejan rooms as well as a large collection of the local ceramic figurines (*boneços de Estremoz*). These brightly coloured, naive models of saints or historical personalities are sometimes arranged into tableaux, a massive *romaria* procession, for instance. Downstairs, across a courtyard, you can watch two local craftsmen producing facsimiles, some of which are for sale.

The much more lively lower part of town spreads itself around the enormous Rossio square. Each Saturday a fair is held here—good for the purchase of pottery—and it also contains a small **Tourist Office** in one of its corners. There is a good pensão, the **Carvalho**, in the nearby Largo de Republica.

Much of Estremoz is built from the white marble quarried locally. Continuing east along the N4, you will discover that the tiny town of nearby **BORBA** also employs the marble, notably in its lavish eighteenth-century fountain and in a series of small chapels dotted around the town. Borba is also known for its good quality red wine.

You pass one of the quarries just a few kilometres south on the way to the town of **VILA VIÇOSA**, another marble town, although something of a disappointment. Its history is closely tied to the Dukes of Bragança whose palace, the **Paço Ducal**, occupies all one side of the Terreiro do Paço. Its classical façade of 1602–3 is in three storeys with pilasters of a different order on each floor. The austerity of its design, reflecting the influence of the country's Spanish occupants, can also be seen on the other side of the square in the church of Santo Agostinho. A much more exhuberant architectural feature is the justly famous Porto dos Nos (Gate of the Knots), originally an entrance to the town and visible from the Borba road. It repeats the Manueline motif, associated with the Bragança family and already

The Porto dos Nos at Vila Viçosa

seen at Évoramonte. It was the eighth Duke of Bragança, later Dom João IV, who led the uprising against the Spanish in 1640 and his equestrian monument stands in the centre of the square. The palace may be visited (though it is closed on Mondays): assemble at the front for a guided tour lasting about an hour. The older part of the town surrounds the castle built by Dom Dinis.

Heading eastwards along a small road takes you, after 11km, to the village of São Romão where you turn right and then 6km on, having reached a larger road, left. From here the town of **JUROMENHA** is just a few kilometres away. It stands on the River Guadiana which here forms the border with Spain. The town is very small and isolated and only its abandoned and decaying castle reveals its former significance as a garrison. You can gain access to the castle by applying for the key (*o chave*) at one of the houses in the main—practically the only—street. It dates back to Roman times but was badly damaged by an explosion in 1659. Two chapels may be found within its walls from which can be seen a long stretch of the peaceful Guadiana river and, beyond the flat Castilian fields, the town of Olivença. Originally part of Portugal, Olivença was captured by the Spanish in 1801 and, despite the 1814 Treaty of Paris which judged it to be Portuguese, it has never been returned.

Returning west along the N373 through flat fertile pastures takes you eventually to another small castle town, **ALENDROAL**. In fact, the road skirts the town and, if you prefer, you can continue south along the N255 (which eventually leads to Reguengos de Monsaraz). Just off this straight road there suddenly appears, after some 10km, yet another border castle town, **Terena**. It is almost as small as Juromenha but with highly recommended accommodation in the shape of a recently restored and very comfortable eighteenth-century house, the **Casa de Terena** (068 451332), less than a hundred yards from the castle walls.

The castle, at Terena, built for Dom João I, fills a gap in the defensive line running from Elvas to Mourão. Later Manueline additions, the keep and alcaide's residence, suggest the work of Diogo de Arruda. The main street, Rua Direita, is lined with a mixture of well-preserved, flower-decked Renaissance and Baroque houses and the whole village is beautifully quiet and serene.

Nearby the unusual fortified Gothic church of Nossa Senhora de Boa Nova probably indicates the site of a settlement pre-dating the castle. The church is close to a lake, Lucefece, where various watersports can be enjoyed.

Continue south from here along the N225 towards **REGUENGOS DE MONSARAZ**, a town which produces a popular, good red wine. To follow our route, however, turn off to the left a few kilometres before you get to Reguengos, taking the small road through the village of Carrapatelo en route for the fortified hill town of **MONSARAZ**. This is an extraordinary medieval town, self-contained and perfectly preserved; though thoroughly 'discovered' by tourism, it is well worth visiting. You can walk round the streets of the town in less than four minutes but there are four churches including the large Santa Maria da Lagoa which contains a particularly fine thirteenth-century tomb (that of Gomes Martins). This is in the central main square, which also houses the **Tourist Office**, an unusual *pelourinho* and a fifteenth-century house (now a museum) containing an original fresco depicting 'Good and Bad Government'. Historically, the town's prosperity was due to its protection by the Templars and later the Order of Christ, but as a settlement it is very much older and the lands which surround it are rich in prehistoric remains.

The cromlech of Xarez near Monsaraz

Close by is the carved **Menhir of Bulhoa**, the large phallic **Menhir of Outeiro** and the **Cromlech of Xarez**, a circle of some fifty stones surrounding a phallic menhir. It was discovered in 1969 and is thought to have been used for fertility rituals. It can be found on your left soon after leaving Monsaraz along the small road which joins the N256.

When you reach the N256 turn left, then almost immediately cross the Guadiana river before reaching **MOURÃO**, 5km further on. After the magic of Monsaraz this is an anticlimax despite the town's castle.

More interesting is the agricultural town of **MOURA**, 35km to the south along the N386. The Moors called the town Al-Manijah; its later name, Moura (which means Moorish girl) derives from the legend of its recapture by Christian forces in 1166. On the day planned for her wedding, Salukia, daughter of the local governor, opened the town gates to what she thought was her bridegroom, Brafama, and his retinue. In fact, it was a party of Christian knights who, having ambushed and killed her betrothed, proceeded to capture the town. Either from fear or from grief, Salukia threw herself from the tower of the castle. The story is commemorated in the town's coat of arms despite lack of any historical evidence of its authenticity. A real Moorish presence is comparatively well represented here in the narrow streets of the *Mouraria*, a short walk from the main square, where one of the low white houses is now a small museum displaying recently found stonework with Arabic inscriptions. The south-eastern gates of the castle also reveal residual Arab elements but most of the castle dates from the rebuilding ordered by Dom Dinis following Castile's eventual recognition of the town as Portuguese in 1295.

Opposite the castle is the church of São João Baptista, with an impressive Manueline portal. When we entered the church, Mass was in progress so we saw little but heard, from the congregation, some of the enthusiastic singing for which this part of the Alentejo is famous. Moura also has a reputation for good quality olive oil and this can be purchased from the large market building also in the main square. The **Tourist Office** is nearby, as is the **Hotel de Moura** (85 22494) and the cheaper **Pensão Alentejana** (85 22529).

4 BAIXO ALENTEJO AND THE ALGARVE

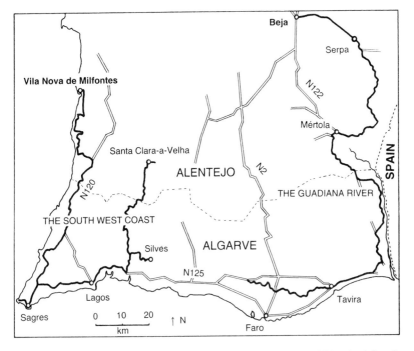

The lands west of the Guadiana river (including part of North Africa) were called by the Muslim occupants of the peninsula 'al-Gharb al-Andalus' (the west of Andalus): hence the name 'Algarve'. With the **Baixo Alentejo**, the **Algarve** contains the greatest evidence of the 540-year Muslim presence in this part of the country. Few buildings remain: the magnificent castle at Silves, and parts of a mosque at Mértola. What lasted longer was the Muslim contribution to the development of agriculture and husbandry. They improved irrigation by introducing the bucket wheel (*nora*) which could draw water from deep wells (an example survives at Serpa). They introduced and cultivated new plants (rice, oranges and saffron) and established the large-scale production of almonds and figs which has continued to this day. The blossoming of the almond trees in early spring is one of the province's most spectacular sights.

Moorish influence can also be seen in the domestic architecture of villages and towns which is similar to that of North Africa. Houses are whitewashed throughout the south and roof terraces can be found in the Barrocal, or limestone region, just north of the coastal strip. But the most spectacular element of the Algarvian house is the traditional chimney, whose lantern-like top often displays highly elaborate fretwork.

The Guadiana River

3 days/200km/from Beja to Loulé

It is not difficult to understand the attraction of the southern part of the peninsula for the Moors. Much of it really feels like a more temperate extension of North Africa. Following the Guadiana takes you through sparsely populated farm land where the main crops are citrus fruits. As you pass from the Alentejo into the Algarve the only noticeable difference is the greater proportion of visitors to local people, resulting from the unfortunate over-development of the coast as a centre for mass tourism.

BEJA, the capital of Baixo Alentejo, rises from the surrounding wheat-growing plains and is dominated by its vast and solid *torre de menagem* built onto the city walls by Dom Dinis. The castle occupies the site where the ancient *castrense* fortification stood when the Romans invaded the country. It was here that Julius Caesar made peace with the Lusitanian tribes, hence the choice of a new name, Pax Julia, which the Moors later shortened to Beja.

The town was first occupied by the Moors in 713 and was known as a centre of culture and learning before Christian attempts to retake it. In the second half of the twelfth century it changed hands several

The torre de menagem *at Beja*

times, and it was eventually refortified, by command of Dom Afonso III, in 1252. The great tower may be visited (but not on Mondays); it is similar to the one at Estremoz but with refinements, such as the angled balconies near the top of each corner. You will have to climb 183 steps, via three

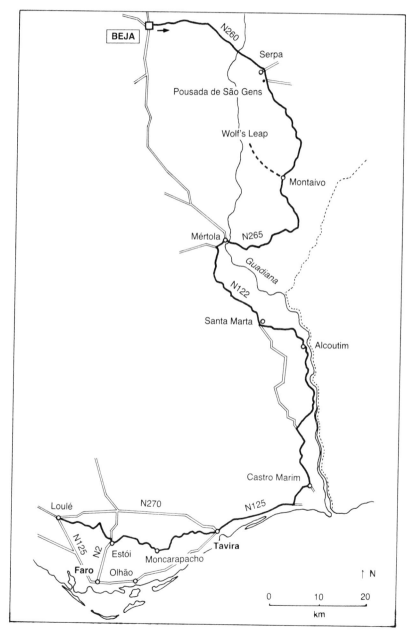

vaulted chambers, to reach the battlements and a view of the vast plain stretching into the distance.

Nearby is the church of Santo Amaro, one of the few in Portugal to contain remnants from pre-Moorish times. Its main Visigothic features are the decorated columns and capitals of the interior.

In the Largo de Duques de Beja stands the former Convento de Nossa Senhora de Conceição, chiefly famous as the home of Sister Mariana Alcofardo and now the **Regional Museum** (closed Sundays). In 1669, Sister Mariana's empassioned letters to the man who had abandoned her, the Chevalier de Chantilly, were published in France. As *Love Letters of a Portuguese Nun*, their popularity led to many editions despite doubts about their authenticity. The convent contains much of interest including a sumptuous Baroque chapel, a cloister and chapter house lined with some remarkable *azulejos* from the sixteenth century and earlier.

In 1962, a military uprising against the Salazar regime was organised here by General Humberto Delgado. It was unsuccessful and three years later, near Badajoz, just over the Spanish border, Delgado was assassinated.

The **Residencial Coelho** (084 24032) and the **Pensão Tomas** (084 24613) are both central and the latter has a good restaurant.

About 28km south east along the N260, you reach **SERPA**, quiet and clean like many Alentejan towns. Here, the painted trim of the whitewashed houses is pale grey, adding to the slightly ghostly serenity that prevails. Because of its proximity to the border, it is a fortified town. Alfonso X of Castile laid claim to it after the Almohads were driven out in 1232, but these claims were settled only when his daughter, Brites, married Dom Afonso II. Much of the city wall remains and along part of it, next to the Porta de Beja, is an old aqueduct fed by a large *nora* or well of the type introduced by the Moors. In the centre of town, in the Praça de Republica, the **Restaurante Alentejano** is a good place to eat; and nearby, up some steps, is the church of Santa Maria. Cross the largo in front of the church and go through an old arch, and you will come to the mansion house of the Marquis de Ficalho, built into the castle walls in the seventeenth century.

Heading out of town towards the village of Santa Iria, and eventually Mértola, takes you past the modern **Pousada de São Gens** (084 52327), well situated on a small hill overlooking the surrounding plains. In fact, as you head south along the N265, the prevailing flatness is broken up by several small hills. At **MONTAIVO**, if you are making good time, turn right onto an unsurfaced road and after a twenty minute drive through farm land you reach a spot where you leave the car and walk down to the Ribeira de Limas, a tributary of the river Guadiana. At this particular spot, the water is forced through a narrow course of schist forming a powerful and spectacular torrent of water which falls about 50m. A wolf, escaping from hunters, is said to have leapt from one side to the other (just credible), hence the name of the spot, **Pulo do Lobo**, Wolf's Leap.

After retracing your route to Montaivo, continue south on the N265. In the 17km between the Barragem da Tapada Grande and Mértola the landscape becomes more barren and mountainous. As you approach, you will see the white town of **MÉRTOLA** in the distance set on a hill on the far side of the Guadiana river which you cross by a modern bridge. To the Romans this was the river Anas; the Moors called it the Wadi-Anas, which was corrupted to the present Guadiana.

In spite of 500 years of Muslim occupation, Mértola is the only town in the whole country where definite traces of a mosque have survived. Inside the whitewashed parish church the square plan and columns suggest former use as a Muslim place of worship and this has been confirmed by the discovery of a *mihrab* (a niche indicating the direction of Mecca) and a horseshoe arch just above what is now the sacristy door.

The church nestles at the foot of the ruined castle which contains remnants of both Roman and Moorish masonry. The keep dates from 1292 after the town had been entrusted to the Order of Saint Iago in return for its help during the reconquest.

The Romans called the town Myrtilis; it was important because of its situation midway between Beja and Seville and because the river, navigable to just beyond this point, made it a useful inland port. A little way downstream are the remains of a jetty-like structure built of Roman materials but probably at a later date. The charm of Mértola, like many 'forgotten' Alentejan towns, lies in its peacefulness and its great views of the river along which the brilliant white houses spread themselves.

The church—formerly a mosque—at Mértola

Leave town, heading west, and after about 2km turn left onto the N122, which eventually reaches the Algarve coast at Vila Real de Santo António. As you travel south the terrain becomes increasingly bare, in many parts relieved only by the ever present *Cistus* (rock rose) shrub. After about 22km you cross into the Algarve. Passing by the village of Santa Marta, turn left and head west for the small town of **ALCOUTIM**. This is another 'lost' town situated, like Mértola, on the Guadiana which, from here all the way to the sea, forms the border with Spain. There is little to do here except explore the thirteenth-century castle (both churches were closed when we visited), or sit by the river and look across to Spain and the equivalent, slightly larger, town of Sanlucar de Guadiana, also with a castle.

The road heading south from Alcoutim is little used, and for about 15km provides an undisturbed meander along the river bank as far as Foz de Odeleite where you turn right and eventually rejoin the N122. Another 14km, as you near the river estuary, takes you to the town of **CASTRO MARIM**. This was the original headquarters of the Order of Christ, established here by Dom Dinis as protection against the threat of attack from the Moors. Their huge castle disintegrated after they left for Tomar in 1334. Dom João IV rebuilt it along with a new fortress on the opposite hill but both were badly damaged in the 1755 earthquake. Today the town is sandwiched between the two ruins.

Rather than continuing south at this point, head west from Castro Marim, a detour that connects you to the coast road (N125) but bypasses Vila Real de Santo António. This part of the journey is not very picturesque, being dotted with a mixture of speculative tourist facilities and light industrial sites. However, **TAVIRA**, reached after about 18km, has managed to remain the most handsome of the Algarvian coastal towns in spite of destruction in 1755 and a recent massive increase in tourism. In the centre of town many of the older houses display some distinctive architectural features, notably unusual pyramidal tiled roofs and window shutters and doors of elaborate wooden lattice-work. There are also several fine churches, although access may be difficult. Santa Maria do Castelo, near the remains of the castle, was possibly built on the site of mosque and preserves a Gothic doorway dating from the time of the Christian reconquest of the town in 1239. Inside is the tomb of Paio Peres Correa, the commander of the Christian forces.

Tavira's prosperity declined as the river silted up but it is still an important centre for tunny fishing. The busiest part of town is along the river Gilão near the old bridge, badly damaged by the floods of 1989. There is no shortage of places to stay. The **Pensão Lagoas** (081 22252) is recommended and the **Imperial** restaurant is good but often crowded.

As you leave Tavira, take the main road to Faro and then immediately afterwards, the first road on your right marked to São Estevão. This is a small country lane which will take you through orchards of orange, almond and medlar trees. The medlar is common in Portugal: the fruit is about 5cm long, ripens in early summer, and should be eaten when very ripe after peeling away the thin yellow skin.

Once in São Estevão, follow the road marked to Luz and after passing the cemetery take the turning to Estiramantes and then continue on to Moncarapacho. As you approach the town you will see a sign on your right and (after 0.5km) another sign to the Serra de São Miguel at which point you turn left. At 410m, this mountain commands a view over the coastal towns of Tavira, Olhão and Faro. From here continue along an unsurfaced road (to be avoided if wet), via **AZINHEIRO**. This village gives you a good idea of the old Algarve of small white houses with their water tanks and massive, elaborately decorated chimneys.

From Azinheiro the road, tarmacked once again, leads to **ESTÓI**. The main reason for visiting this pretty whitewashed village is to gain access to the gardens of the **Palácio de Estói**. In the south grand country houses are rare and this one, built in the late eighteenth century, has not been lived in for many years. It is now owned by the local council and the garden is open to the public. It is worth a visit, being a highly exotic, but classically-inspired fantasy, effectively employing a mixture of ornamentation (mainly *azulejos* and statuary) to create a series of almost theatrical tableaux. The Roman-looking columns are precisely that, taken from the nearby site at **Milreu**, a little way west of the village just off the main road. Once a Roman town called Ossonoba, the site contains part of a temple, later converted into a church, as well as third-century baths decorated with mosaics.

Leaving the N32 at Milreu, head west along a small country road which will eventually take you, after some 10km, to **LOULÉ**. Every year, at the beginning of March, the town holds a carnival in celebration of the blossoming of the almond. This festival is known as **The Battle of the Flowers** and includes parades, music and much dancing in the streets. Another attraction is the busy Moorish-style market, held every Sunday, where you can buy some of the locally produced baskets made from esparto grass or strips of palm. Loulé is also a centre for craftsmen working in metal. Behind the market is the thirteenth-century church, igreja matriz, whitewashed, with a tall bell-tower and containing some fine *azulejos*. Of all the Algarvian small towns, Loulé possesses the best selection of decorated chimneys. Just 2km outside the town at the **Monte da Piedade** there is a shrine whose image of the Virgin is carried down into the town on Easter Sunday and sheltered in the church of São Fransisco. After 15 days, it is returned to the shrine in a great procession by eight men who carry it on a heavy float. This *romaria* is named after the Mãe Soberana or Sovereign Mother and is thought to be an ancient pagan festival that has become Christianised.

There are several places to stay in Loulé, including the **Pensão Iberica** (089 62027).

The South West Coast

3 days/220km/from Milfontes to the Santa Clara reservoir

This stretch of coastline, especially along the Alentejo, has managed to remain unspoilt by the increase in tourism. It offers long stretches of sandy beaches uncluttered by insensitive tourist facilities. Perhaps that is why it is mainly visitors from Lisbon that take advantage of it. Its only disadvantages are the strength of the Atlantic breakers, which can often make swimming an impossibility, and the occasional fierceness of the wind.

About 40km south of Sines at the mouth of the River Mira stands the town of **VILA NOVA DE MILFONTES**. Before the advent of tourism, the most frequent visitors to this part of the coastline were North African pirates and, in 1552, the old Moorish fortress had to be rebuilt to protect the town against their attacks. The fortress, **O Castelo**, is now an unusual but expensive place to stay (083 96108). There are also several *pensões* nearby and it is possible to rent rooms in private houses.

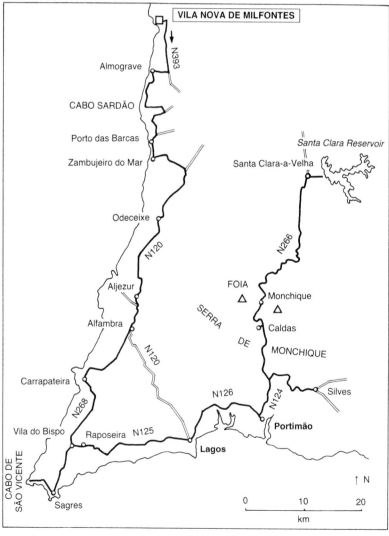

Vila Nova de Milfontes spreads itself along the northern bank of the river and most of its houses are the small *alentejano* type, white with blue or yellow around the windows and doors. The beach is particularly popular, as you can swim in the river, practise windsurfing and canoeing or even brave the powerful waves of the sea itself. For this the beach on the southern bank is the most suitable. You reach it by returning to the main road, crossing the bridge and then taking the small road on your right. From here, continue along the main road to the right for the beach of **Almograve**. Ten kilometres further south is the lighthouse of **Cabo Sardão** where the cliffs plunge sharply into the sea. At this point the road heads back inland before reaching another junction, where you turn right and pass through the villages of Touril, Porto das Barcas and, finally, **ZAMBUJEIRA DO MAR**. This is a small, charming, cliff-top town, whose coves and sandy beaches are particularly favoured by young Lisboetas. The town itself is just a line of houses along the main road but with no accommodation available.

To continue down the coast from Zambujeira first go back to the main road by heading inland, then turn right at the first junction (crossing the border between the Alentejo and the Algarve at Odeceixe). After 16km you will reach **ALJEZUR**, an old Arab town, whose name means 'old village of the bridges'. The Ribeira de Cerca, once a navigable stream, flows down from the hills of Monchique. In the late eighteenth century the river had become so blocked with silt that the water stagnated and it was decided that the town should be moved to a healthier, higher location to the east. A new church was built but not many houses. Most of the town remained on the original site, where the ruins of the old castle still stand.

You are now in the **Algarve** and, although the houses are still small, their colours have changed to greens, pinks and blues. Already among these are some of the typical terraced white houses with their characteristic chimneys. The narrow cobbled streets tend to be a little less immaculate than in the neighbouring province but the small town is still very quiet and remote from the tourist life of the southern beaches; as you walk to the top of the hill, you can often smell the fresh bread being baked on one of the communal outdoor ovens.

Take the right fork at Alfambra, 7km south of Aljezur, towards the coast. The beaches along this stretch of coastline are all of great beauty but the one which stands out is the beach of **Carrapateira**, just off the small village of the same name. There are no hotels in the village but many people are willing to rent rooms and even entire houses. To the north is the beach of **Bordeira**, a vast expanse of sand that eventually turns into dunes. To the south is the equally long **Praia do Arado**, bordered by cliffs. It is not advisable to camp anywhere near these beaches as the local police regularly check to see that this does not occur.

About 14km after Carrapateira you arrive at **VILA DO BISPO** (Town of the Bishop). Originally called Santa Maria do Cabo, its name was changed after Dom Manuel I offered it to the bishopric of the Algarve. It is a very quiet place today with just a couple of bars and a restaurant, O

Moinho, named after the windmills at the north of the town. Continue south along the N268 to reach Sagres.

SAGRES will always be associated with the name of the Infante Dom Henrique, a controversial figure about whom opinions are divided. He was the third son of Dom João I and Philippa of Lancaster who later became the governor of the Order of Christ. He is considered by some to be the most important figure in the development of navigational science, which in turn led to Portuguese imperial expansion and power. His brother, Dom Pedro, granted him the town of Tercanaabale (now Cabo São Vicente) with its adjacent land, including Sagres. Here, and at his farm at Raposeira, about 12km inland, he spent most of his life.

Sagres has a certain air of mystery about it; there seems to be a permanent stillness, even in the liveliest bar. This muted atmosphere is enhanced by the cold winds that invariably blow all year round and by the hazy mist. The focal point of the town is the fortress, which may have been the famous Escola Nautica where Dom Henriques gathered together scientists, map-makers and seafarers from all over the world. Recent excavations have uncovered a great stone compass. Measuring 43m in diameter, it points in 32 directions and would seem to date from the time of the Infante. Unfortunately, all the records of the School were destroyed when Sir Francis Drake, at the command of Queen Elizabeth I, attacked Sagres, Beliche and Cabo São Vicente. A map showing what the fortress was like is in the British Museum but not even ruins now remain from that era. The fortress's design was completely changed and it was rebuilt, only to be destroyed yet again by the earthquake of 1755, when the sea receded 3km, forming a tidal wave that reached the top of the cliffs.

Before the time of the Escola Nautica, Sagres was mainly used as a shelter for boats prevented by bad weather from rounding the perilous Cabo São Vicente. Today it is very much a tourist town, especially in summer during the Sagres Music Festival, usually held at the beginning of August. Accommodation is plentiful and the **Pousada do Infante** (082 64222) is on the site of Dom Henriques's former residence.

Further along this road is the most popular beach at Sagres, the **Praia do Beliche**. This is the point from where the explorers' caravels, bearing the red cross of the Order of Christ on their sails, set off on their expeditions. Nearby, on the cliffs stands the fortress of **Beliche**, the lookout post for the bay. It was rebuilt in 1632, following its destruction by Drake's fleet, and contains a small church dedicated to St Catherine. More impressive is Cabo São Vicente itself; the cape was called the Sacrum Promotorium even before the body of the martyr, St Vincent was brought here from Valencia. A hermitage was built out of rough stones, which the Visigoths later enlarged and this became known as the Temple of the Crow. Edresi, an Islamic geographer, claimed that there were ten crows permanently watching over the temple and that the priests always received foreigners with hospitality. The body of the saint was later taken to Lisbon (see p. 16).

Away from the political intrigues of Lisbon, the Cape was a place for meditation and thought, as well as ideal for meeting travellers who could exchange and provide information. It is currently thought that while the School was situated in Sagres, the Palace of the Infante was here at Cabo São Vicente. In the waters off the Cape, the French Admiral Tourville defeated the Anglo-Dutch fleet in 1693, and later Lord Jervis and Admiral Nelson won an important battle against the Spanish in these same waters.

Leave Sagres by the same road as you entered it, once again passing Vila do Bispo. Continue on the main road (N125) and you will drive past **RAPOSEIRA**, about half way (4km) to Figueira. On the left is the unique Romanesque church of Our Lady of Guadalupe, probably built by the Order of the Templars in the thirteenth century. Especially interesting are the stone carvings on the columns of the chapels, depicting oak and palm leaves and human faces.

LAGOS was once a quiet fishing village, and of all the tourist resorts in the Algarve, it has best managed to retain its original charm. If you are driving in from Sagres you approach Lagos from the top and follow the main road round the fortress and down to the harbour. The centre of town is accessible only to pedestrians.

Along these narrow streets, bars and restaurants proliferate. The Algarve is a fish-eating region but, with the influx of tourism, many of the old *tascas*, where you could have sardines grilled on charcoal fires placed outside the main door, have given way to English fish and chip shops. There are still a few good fish restaurants, however, especially along the riverside. This is also a good place to try some of the special *algarvio* sweets. There are two main varieties: those made with figs and those made with almonds. The former can be either plain figs stuffed with nuts or a fig paste mixed with chocolate and shaped into animals or baskets. The almond sweets are either made from dry marzipan, shaped into flowers, fruits or vegetables—almost too pretty to eat—or they are made with eggs, for example the famous Dom Rodrogo, sweet and gooey and wrapped in silver paper.

Lagos is closely linked with the name of Dom Sebastião and it is his statue, by the Portuguese sculptor, José Cutileiro, that stands in the main square of the town. In 1557, at the age of three, Sebastião became king on the death of his grandfather. The young monarch was brought up by his grandmother and his uncle, Cardinal Dom Henriques. He suffered from poor health and was more interested in hunting and riding than in his studies. His great dream was to lead a crusade to Africa, which he twice attempted. The second time, in 1578, he enlisted an army of 17,000 from all over Portugal and Spain, and left for North Africa from Lagos. He was seeking a confrontation with the Sultan Mulaie Almelique and headed for the interior where he died in combat at the Battle of Alcácer-Kibir, leaving the nobility depleted and the country bankrupt and kingless. Only *sebastianismo* remains; the belief that one day the King will return to deliver Portugal from all its misfortunes.

Most of the town was destroyed in the 1755 earthquake but some parts of the aqueduct and of the sixteenth century wall have survived. So has the chapel of Santo António, in the main Praça de Republica, whose exuberant interior contains much gilded woodwork and highly decorative *azulejos* all dating from the early eighteenth century. As patron saint of the Lagos regiment (though born in Lisbon) St Antony was given the status of a soldier before being promoted to captain by Dom Pedro II, with an appropriate increase in salary. Also in the square is the Custom House under whose arches the first modern slave market was set up in 1441. Lagos was the birth place of Gil Eanes, the first Portuguese navigator to round Cape Bojador.

Close to Lagos is a magnificent stretch of beach called **Meia Praia** whose great rocks, sculpted by the sea, have exotic names like the Giant of the Bay and the Doll. The best way to see them is to hire a boat, either in **Ponte da Piedade** or at the beach of **Dona Ana**. The trip takes about an hour and takes you through caves and to small beaches with beautiful clear, green water.

When you leave Lagos, take the road (still N125) to Portimão, but just before you reach it (after about 16km) take the N124 on your left towards Monchique. You will thus avoid the great traffic jams that during the summer sometimes add as much as two hours to the journey across the town.

On your right after about 7km the N124 bears right to Silves, another 10km away, where the beautiful red sandstone castle is definitely worth a visit. A few kilometres ahead, just before you reach the Riviera do Odelouca, there is a restaurant called **Oriq** on your right. This is a particularly pleasant place to stop for lunch in the summer, as you can sit outside in the shade of the eucalyptus trees and eat chicken, spare ribs or sardines grilled on a charcoal fire.

SILVES was one of the great Moorish towns although a castle already existed from Roman times. The Moors transformed it into a place of great

Silves is dominated by its beautiful castle

beauty, the 'Alcacer Axarajibe' (the Palace of the Veranda). Xelb, as it was then called, was an important commercial and cultural centre. Most of the inhabitants came from the Yemen and kept the Arabic language pure even though, by the twelfth century, the Moroccan *almohads* had gained political dominion over the peninsula.

The Christian reconquest of Silves by Dom Sancho I was assisted by German, Danish and English crusaders en route to the Holy Land. Their over-zealousness led to the city's plunder and when the offer of money failed to make them leave, the Portuguese were forced to drive them away. Two years later the Moors regained control of the area and it was not until 1249 that it finally succumbed to the army of Dom Afonso III, thus establishing the boundaries of the country as they have stood to this day.

Silves maintained its importance until the river Arade ceased to be navigable and the castle became almost completely ruined following several earthquakes. It was rebuilt in 1940 and contains a great cistern from Moorish times, as well as underground silos and a crematorium. In summer, there is a Beer Festival, when the streets of the town overflow with tourists. In winter, however, it is rather quiet.

As you drive into Silves, follow the course of the river, rather than heading immediately into the town centre. At the last roundabout turn left into the town, park your car as soon as possible and walk back to the roundabout. Here, on the left hand side, is a cross known as the Cruz de Portugal, a sixteenth-century limestone monument, with Christ on the Cross on one side and the Descent from the Cross on the other. Then carry on driving uphill and you will reach the square with the entrance to the castle and the old Gothic cathedral.

The Cathedral of Silves was built in 1189 and then rebuilt in 1242. It was the chief cathedral of the Algarve until the sixteenth century. Much of the church has been changed by subsequent decoration but inside you can still appreciate the striking red colour of the Silves sandstone. There are some interesting tombs in a side chapel that the verger informed us were those of local sailors.

To reach Monchique, drive back to the main road junction, where you should turn right onto the N266. This winding road takes you up to the Serra de Monchique. **CALDAS DE MONCHIQUE** is the first village on your left where the spa is situated, surrounded by elegant houses from the turn of the century.

The highest point of the *serra* is **Foia** (902m). The name derives from the rock *foiaite* that erupted above the schist layer. This is the highest point of the Algarve and from here, on a clear day, you can see outlined a great stretch of the coast. To reach it you make a sharp turn to your left when you reach the main square in the town of **MONCHIQUE**, a few kilometres north of Caldas. The town itself is worth exploring, however. By taking the narrow, steep street to the right of the Fire Station and then taking the second turning on your right, you will reach the *igreja matriz*, with a Manueline portal.

There are several pensões but we advise you to drive on to the **Pousada de Santa Clara** (083 52250) near **Belha**, 32km north. Although its architecture is not particularly striking, the view it commands over the great **reservoir of Santa Clara** is spectacular. This is the largest reservoir in Portugal and its clear water collected from the Mira river is used for irrigation purposes only. This river, which joins the sea at Vila Nova de Milfontes, is rich in fish such as perch and bass. It is a popular place for water-skiing and boats may be hired.

5 TRÁS-OS-MONTES

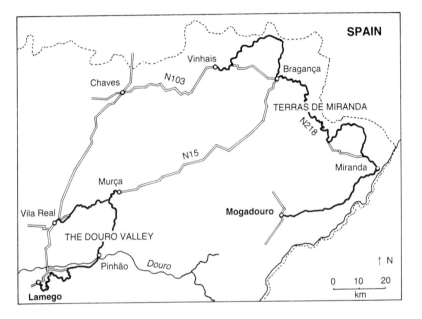

This is the most remote and isolated province in Portugal: behind the mountains (which is what *trás-os-montes* means) and hemmed in on its northern and eastern sides by Spain. With the exception of the Douro valley, the terrain is rugged and difficult to cultivate and, despite communally organised farming in many villages, it has a long history of emigration. The climate is also harsher and more extreme than the neighbouring Minho region and winters can be fierce, especially in the far north east. This has made the Transmontanas, whose way of life has remained fundamentally unchanged for centuries, a tough and self-reliant people. Many of them trace their ancestry back to the Celts and it is quite usual, but still startling, to come across villagers with blond hair and blue or green eyes. Several old traditions have survived, such as the *Paulito* dance still seen around Miranda, accompanied by drums and bagpipes, the only region where this instrument exists. Few travellers venture this far but to be put off by its harsh reputation would be a mistake. Trás-os-

Montes has a unique and varied beauty, from the jagged mountains of the Serra de Mogadouro to the flat, boulder-strewn lands between Miranda and Bragança.

The Douro Valley
2–3 days/140km/from Lamego

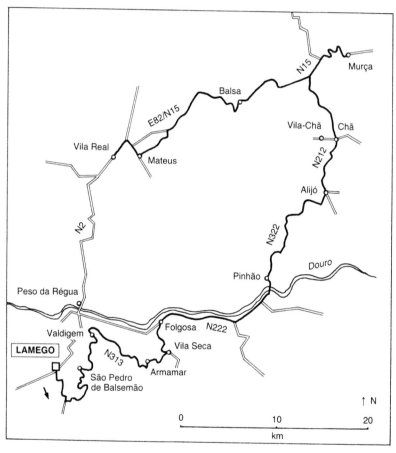

Although this route is for the most part in Trás-os-Montes, it begins in the Beira Alta province, south of the Douro river. The region along the river valley, demarcated from Lamego to the Spanish border, is so rich in vineyards that it has become known as the País do Vinho (Land of Wine). The scale of cultivation is impressive, especially when you realise that the slaty soil is not very fertile, the summers are often scorchingly hot and the steep hills make the building of stone wall terraces a necessity. Not all the wine is used for the production of port; many good table wines can also be found, of which the best is Barca Velha.

LAMEGO does not really live up to its reputation as one of the north's most exquisite small towns. It is true that there are several fine baroque town houses (particularly the eighteenth-century Casa das Brolhas) and some good churches, but the town feels dirty and uncared for, and its outskirts have recently been marred by some badly planned additions. It is an old town: the Visigoth King Sisebuto minted his coinage here and the town was central to a border dispute between the Caliphate and the Kingdom of Asturias in 877. It was reconquered from the Moors by Fernando I ('the Great') of León and Castile in 1057. The castle, on a hill near the centre of town, dates from this period but apart from its thirteenth-century keep (now seemingly occupied by boy scouts) and a water cistern (difficult to get at) little remains.

The town's main thoroughfare, the Avenida Visconde Guedes Teixeira, where you can find the **Tourist Office** and several over-priced *pensões*, runs from the Praça de Camões, next to the cathedral, to the steps leading to Lamego's most famous monument, the pilgrimage church of Nossa Senhora dos Remédios (Our Lady of Remedies). After climbing about 650 steps (on your knees if you are a sufficiently devout pilgrim), you finally reach the slightly crude Rococo church, more interesting outside than in. Like many pilgrimage churches, its building and embellishment has progressed according to the generosity of the pilgrims who flock here for the spectacular *romaria* between 6 and 8 September, so that, although begun in 1748, one of the towers is nineteenth-century and the bottom flight of steps was completed as recently as 1962. Though Lamego was made a diocese in 1071, little is left of the cathedral of that period apart from a twelfth-century belfry. Its highly decorated, late Gothic, west portico is particularly fine, as is the Renaissance cloister on its north side, but most of the interior, remodelled in the eighteenth century by Nasoni, the architect of the Solar de Mateus (see p. 76), is not in good condition.

Next to the cathedral, in the former bishop's palace, there is a good museum, whose exhibits are well laid out but badly labelled. The main altar-piece from the cathedral is now housed here: five panels attributed to Vasco Fernandes (known as Grão Vasco (Great Vasco), an artist active in Viseu in the early fifteenth century) representing the creation of the Animals, the Annunciation, the Visitation, the Presentation in the Temple and the Circumcision. A good place to stay is the **motel** just west of the town on the way up to the Meadas mountains.

We left the town after buying a picnic which included some of the good local smoked ham, turned right by the cathedral and after a short while took the left turn at the church of the Desterro (closed at the time but apparently worth visiting). Following the sign for Balsemão, you rapidly reach the river of the same name and, passing through its valley along a rough but manageable road, arrive at **São Pedro de Balsemão** after about 3.5km. This small Visigoth church is one of the oldest in Portugal, dating from the seventh century. It contains the tomb of Afonso Pires, a fourteenth-century Bishop of Oporto, and a crudely painted but cheery coffered ceiling from the seventeenth-century restoration of the church.

There was hardly anyone about when we were there; just a local family quietly sitting on the steps of the church, gazing at the wooded hills across the river.

Pressing on, the road gets rougher and narrower but not for long; less than 1km away a bridge is reached. Cross it and keep going towards a dam which appears up ahead. Take the lower road for the dam, which you cross. If the water level is low, it is worth stopping to look at the weird, Escher-like criss-cross of steps and walkways running down the length of its corners. The road then starts to climb, quite steeply, until you reach a junction where you follow the sign to Valdigem and quite soon, to your left, you catch glimpses of the River Douro down below in the distance.

At Valdigem, turn right onto the N313, which leads to **ARMAMAR** through high hills on whose terraced slopes vines and fruit trees grow. Armamar has a petrol station, a good view of the wooded valley, and a fine romanesque basilican church, just after which you turn left for **VILA SECA**, some 4km away. This is a small village but one containing some houses very characteristic of this region. They are two-storey and almost always made from granite (the main building material of northern Portugal): the lower storey is used exclusively to house livestock, while the upper storey is for human habitation. Entry is via exterior stone steps leading to a wooden verandah. In Vila Seca some of the upper storeys are made entirely from wood and the roofs are traditionally thatched.

Leave the village the way you entered it and then turn right, gradually descending a winding road towards Folgosa, where you finally meet the **Douro**. This is one of the great rivers of the peninsula, if not Europe. Broad and stately, it is flanked on its northern banks by the great port *quintas*, whose gently rising hills are covered over with a profligate greenery of vines, cut back in late autumn to reveal the colossal intricacy of miles of dry-stone terracing. This is a cultivated and controlled land-scape but astonishingly beautiful. For some distance the road (N222) follows the course of the river, crossing three of its tributaries, the Tedo, the Tavora and the Torto before crossing the great river itself. Still to be seen, although now used more for publicity than transporting the wine, are the *barcos rabelos*, long shallow boats with a large square sail, steered by an enormous rudder from a platform in the stern.

Just before the bridge, you pass the eighteenth-century Quinta do Carvalhal and, straight after crossing it, reach **PINHÃO**, an important commercial centre but not really a town worth spending much time in. Follow the N322 for Alijo and soon the road starts to climb once more. This is the heart of the port wine region, and the road goes by some of the most famous *quintas*, including the Quinta do Noval. Late September is the time for harvesting and some of the grapes are still trodden and fermented in the great granite tanks called *lagares*. In fact, only 40 per cent of the wine of this region is made into port; the rest is drunk as table wine, despite the region being demarcated for that purpose only since 1979.

The next village is Favaios, followed by Granja and then **ALIJÓ**, a pleasant, small town and a good place to stay, despite the lack of any notable monuments. The Largo Bispo de Vizela contains the main church opposite a fountain and an enormous plane tree, planted by the Visconde da Ribeira on 25 November 1856. Nearby is the **Pousada do Barão Forrester** (059 95467), named after the Englishman who did so much to improve the port business in the middle of the nineteenth century. His achievements include mapping the River Douro, for which he was ennobled by a grateful government before drowning in the river in 1862.

Up on the plateau, continuing north along the N212, the landscape begins to change noticeably. The vast and seemingly endless vineyards eventually give way to a wider, rock-strewn terrain. Great boulders of granite stand as if deliberately placed in the middle of fields, as, in some cases, they were, thousands of years ago. Beyond Chã and half a kilometre after the turning for Vilar Chã is one such prehistoric dolmen or *anta*. It stands about 400m along a track through a small thicket of trees, a three-walled chamber of stones with another great slab as a roof. Not much is known about these structures except for the fact that they were collective tombs, foetally-positioned skeletons and personal artifacts having been discovered in some of them. The country then gradually becomes more wooded and, 9km further on, you reach the main Vila Real-Bragança road (N15), where you turn right for Murça.

The dolmen near Vilar da Chã

The use of oxen as beasts of burden is still fairly common in Portugal, especially in the north, and it was on this road that we heard and then saw up ahead of us the steady progress of an ox-drawn cart whose unmistakable, and amazingly loud, rasping sound is caused by the slow turning of its wooden axle. You also often see in the fields in this area a small, round, free-standing building, with an angled roof. This is a *pombal*, or pigeon house.

MURÇA is famous for its stone 'pig', one of 16 to be found in Trás-os-Montes and similar to those at Guisando near Avila in Spain. Their precise date and significance is unknown, but they may have been used as idols in Celtic fertility rites, prior to the Roman occupation. This one stands on a plinth in the middle of a small square near the *igreja matriz* and the *pelourinho*, and opposite a shop where the local cooperative sells its wine by the glass.

Retracing your route back out of Murça takes you (once again) past the Baroque façade of the Misericórdia church, which combines a simple design with some wonderful detailing, then on, over the River Tinhola towards Vila Real. This is still vine-growing country but not as lush as the slopes of the Douro valley and interspersed with small pine forests. It is not unusual to see the resin tapped from the pine trees, traditionally by placing an earthenware pot below incisions in the trunk, although nowadays plastic bags are more common.

This road would take you all the way to Vila Real but about 9km from town you turn left for Mouços and from there continue towards **MATEUS**. The **Solar de Mateus** is probably the most famous private house in the whole of Portugal, largely as a result of its appearance on the label of the immensely popular rosé wine of the same name. The wine, produced by the SOGRAPE Company, is not as indifferent as is sometimes claimed; the house, on the other hand, is a masterpiece. The classic Portuguese Baroque pattern, of white, rendered walls highlighting the

The Solar de Mateus

stone dressings, is here handled with extraordinary delicacy and inventiveness. The relatively simple decoration of the two projecting wings, with their triangular pediments floating above the windows like raised eyebrows, give way to the more exuberant detailing of the entrance within the courtyard. Each corner of the roof bears a large, striped finial, and the front door, reached on the first floor by a double stair, is surmounted by a pedimental screen bearing the coat of arms of Jose Botelho Mourão, first Morgado of Mateus, who commissioned the building. The architect was almost certainly the Florentine, Nicolau Nasoni; the house was completed in 1743, and the chapel added in 1750. It is difficult to get a head-on view of the house's symmetrical design because of the small, rectangular lake built in front of it in 1961. Your ticket permits you to wander through the beautiful, parterred garden, as well as giving you guided access to the chapel and the main suite of rooms at the house's entrance. When visiting it is worth asking about concerts that are sometimes performed here.

On leaving Mateus, turn left and left again, onto the E82/N15, for **VILA REAL**, which you reach after a couple of kilometres. This is the capital of Trás-os-Montes. Enclosed by two rivers, the Corgo and the Cabril, it has been a royal town since it was founded and granted a *foral* (charter) by Dom Afonso III in 1272, although it was under his successor, Dom Dinis, that it was given special rights, including one banning nobles from living within its walls. The town grew during the fifteenth century and there are several old houses on the main street, the Avenida de Carvalho Araujo, including (with outside staircase) No. 19, the home of Diogo Cão, the explorer who found the mouth of the river Congo in 1482. The street is named after the commander of a minesweeper, blown up with his ship in 1918 whilst protecting Portuguese shipping in the Azores. His rather bullish, clench-fisted statue is in the same street, next to the **Tourist Office**.

Vila Real is altogether a livelier town than Lamego, with several attractive, narrow shopping streets immediately behind the Tourist Office. Wedged within the angle where two of these streets join is the Clérigos church, reminiscent of the chapel at Mateus and, indeed, possibly designed by Nasoni. The interior is not very interesting but there are some good *azulejos* showing scenes from the life and ministry of St Peter.

The Travessa São Domingos is a small street next to the cathedral, with several places to stay: we chose the **Residencial São Domingos**, a large and rickety establishment, like an old ship, but cosy and cheap. The cathedral itself is a disappointing hotch-potch: a fourteenth-century Dominican convent built over an earlier church, whose later additions have not improved it. More interesting, down the far end of the Avenida, is the church of São Dinis, with a tiny fourteenth-century chapel, containing two sarcophagi attached to its side. Nearby are splendid views of the town's two rivers.

BISALHÃES, a small village about 3km out of town, is where the area's famous black pottery originates. It may be bought in town, and on some of the roadsides leading out of town, but do not be deterred by people telling you it is no longer made in the village—it is. When we finally got there, we found Sr Machado quietly working at his wheel as he has done, on and off, for sixty years. The kiln is simply a covered hole in the ground and burnt pine needles blacken the clay, which is left unglazed. Many artifacts are made but possibly the most useful are the dishes with pushed-up sides which are used for cooking rice.

You can return to Lamego (38km) on the main road, N2.

Terras de Miranda

3 days/200km/from Mogadouro to Vinhais

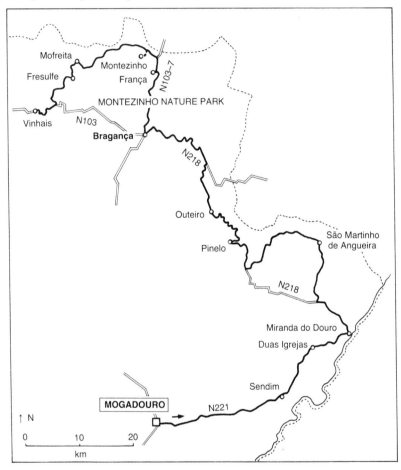

The boulder-strewn moorland between Miranda and Bragança is sparsely populated but not as bleak as sometimes suggested (we travelled in early September which is probably the ideal time). Very few visitors reach this area, which gives it a forgotten feeling but the landscape had a spartan beauty exemplified by the precipitous gorges formed by the Douro at Miranda. Its isolation has meant that much folklore and tradition has survived including the odd local dialect, Mirandés, which is still spoken in some villages. It preserves traces of ancient Leonese as well as containing Hebrew words.

MOGADOURO was a frontier defence against the Spanish, as the remains of its Templar castle show. Now it is a rather more peaceful market town and a pretty enough place in an unspectacular way. The main square has a monument to the town's most famous son, Trindade Coelho (1861–1908), the realist short story writer of peasant life, virtually unknown outside Portugal. There is a fine convent church, São Francisco, containing in its gallery carved stalls and a lectern. The contemporary *igreja matriz* up near the castle is less interesting but from next to the tower there is a good view towards the west. The town was dominated by the Tavora family until the time of Pombal and later on it became an important silk-manufacturing centre but was badly damaged during the Napoleonic wars. Places to stay include the **Pensão Russo** (079 32134) and, just outside the town, the **Residencial São Sebastião** (079 32176).

Mougadouro gives its name to a mountain range but, although high, the countryside from here to Miranda is predominantly flat and open, with large fields containing cereal crops and sometimes cattle. The poplar trees that line the road add to the mildness of the landscape, surprising for a province largely known for its ruggedness and isolation.

Leaving town by the N221, the logical first stop is the village of **SENDIM**, where there is an outstanding restaurant, **Gabrielas**, in front of the church. Another 11km brings you to **DUAS IGREJAS**, the most notable of the small towns or villages in the orbit of Miranda, where the *dança dos paulitos* (stick dance) is still performed. This is one of several ritual dances which exist in the region. It originated as a sword dance and has similarities with English Morris dancing but is rather more spirited. It is danced by pauliteiros—men wearing wide-brimmed, flower-covered hats, coloured silk neckerchiefs, black waistcoats and white embroidered skirts and petticoats. Music is usually provided by one bagpipe (*gaita de foles*) and a pair of drums (*tambores*) and the rhythms and movements can be

extremely complicated. The most reliable time to see a performance here is at festivals, particularly the Feast of the Assumption on 15 August, or in Miranda on 23 August, the Feast of Santa Barbara.

From here it is a mere 7km to **MIRANDA**, situated on the River Douro, which, for about 115km, has been a natural border with Spain (where it is called the Duero). At this point, the river passes through a steep and rocky gorge (the **Pousada de Santa Caterina** (073 42362) looks directly into it) and, if you are lucky, you can sometimes see golden eagles wheeling round and round in the distance. Miranda is a town whose fortune

Pauliteiros (stick dancers) at Duas Igrejas

and prosperity has fluctuated dramatically over the centuries. It was the centre of the church in Tras-os-Montes from 1547 and a few years after this the grand but austere cathedral was begun in a style which reflects the closeness of Spain, despite being built some 30 years before unification of the two countries. Inside is a bizarre object of devotion, *Menino Jesus da Cartolinha* (Boy Jesus of the Opera Hat), a little doll in a glass case with several changes of outfit but always wearing the same top hat.

In 1762, the disadvantage of proximity to the Spanish was proven by their decision to invade the province. Although the invasion was quite quickly repelled, the castle at Miranda was blown up with the loss of about 400 lives. The old walled town, the *costanilho*, has changed little since then. What development there is has sprung up just across the Aranda de Duero bridge and caters for the increasing number of, mainly Spanish, visitors taking advantage of the newish road in order to purchase cheaper goods than at home. The Rua 1 de Maio contains the **Tourist Office** and several *pensões* and there is a good restaurant, **O Mirandés**, nearby which serves the local speciality, *Posta a Mirandes*, a tender steak served with chips.

Miranda's decline resulted in the bishopric being transferred north to its rival, Bragança, in 1782 and that is the direction you now take along the N218. Once again the landscape is tranquil and very beautiful, with gently rolling hills and large open fields. We decided to follow the line of the border with Spain, by taking the road right at the sign for Nossa Senhora de Nazo and then continuing on to **São Martinho de Angueira**. In these remoter regions, visitors are still relatively rare and it is usual to be stared at with an intense, but unaggressive, curiosity. Many of the villages look as though they have changed little for hundreds of years, apart from the occasional repairs that employ modern building materials.

After crossing the River Angueira, you continue west, and then south, for some 15km before joining the main road (now the N218–2). When we were travelling, in October, many areas in the north had been hit by fires following the long, dry summer and, on this road, we witnessed the rapid destruction of a small copse and a field as we drove past, the thick column of smoke visible for miles around. Much of the land is uncultivated but for a few olive trees, since the population is small and supports itself through small freeholdings. What does grow here in plentiful supply is the *estevas* or *Cistus* (rock rose) shrub. We also had regular sightings of birds of prey hovering over the fields, most frequently red kites (*Milvus milvus*), common in Portugal but rare in Britain. The road becomes very windy as you travel through the valley of the River Maças prior to reaching **OUTEIRO**, a small village containing the remains of a border castle and the substantial seventeenth-century (it looks earlier) Cristo church. This has a magnificent exterior with an unusual gallery on its south side and fine façade whose decoration looks Spanish.

Another 10km further on, turn left on to the road from the border and, after crossing the Rio das Igrejas just before Gimond (with the remains of a

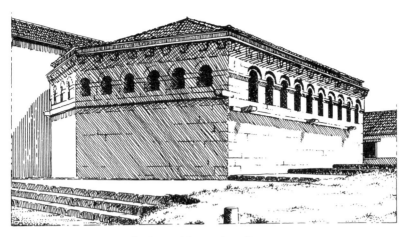

The Domus Municipalis at Bragança

medieval bridge to your right), you can see **BRAGANÇA**, only 7km away, its castle silhouetted against the sky. This is a much more flourishing and lively town than Miranda, not surprisingly, since its population is almost twice as big. The town gives its name to the Ducal family who ruled Portugal from 1640 to 1910, beginning with Dom João IV whose daughter, Catherine, married Charles II of England in 1662. By this time, the family's connection with the town was tenuous. The enclosed medieval town is self-contained and separate from the later town. Its magnificently preserved castle now houses a military museum but of equal interest is the small but imposing Romanesque **Domus Municipalis** (town hall), a rare example of a twelfth-century civic building built to an irregular plan above a cistern. If it is closed, keys may be borrowed from the house opposite. Also in the old town is another transmontana Bronze Age 'pig', similar to the one at Murça but here used as the base for the *pelhourino*.

Two of the roads which approach the old town, Ruas Serpa Pinta and Trindade Coelho, have some good old houses and both of them lead to the Largo de São Vicente, which contains the **Tourist Office** and the church of São Vicente. According to legend, Inês de Castro and Dom Pedro were secretly married here (see p. 30). The tiles on the exterior commemorate not this but Gomes Merevelda's successful rallying of popular resistance against the French occupiers in 1808. Inside, there is a rather alarming ceiling of Christ's Resurrection and the four Evangelists, painted by a local artist at the end of the last century.

We stayed in the **Pensão Rucha** (073 22672), where the landlady proudly showed us her typical transmontana kitchen, an open cooking area on the floor, surrounded by benches, with hams and onions hanging from the ceiling.

Bragança and its environs are one of the best documented regions in Portugal, due almost entirely to one man, Francisco Alves, the abbot of nearby Baçal, who died in 1947 having devoted his life to investigating the lost history and customs of the area. The museum named after him and housed in the former Bishop's Palace, contains archaeological remains, including yet more granite pigs, as well as examples of local crafts and costumes.

One of the most fascinating stories to come to light at the beginning of this century concerns the dispersal of the Jews, following their forced conversion at the hands of Dom Manuel I in 1497. Prior to that, Jews had been relatively well treated by successive Portuguese monarchs, so that as many as 150,000 Spanish Jews sought refuge in Portugal, fleeing across the border from Spain after their expulsion by Ferdinand and Isabella in 1492. They paid substantial amounts of money to stay, and hoped for tolerance but even as New Christians or *Conversos* (*Marrano* is the abusive term, meaning swine) they were both persecuted and prevented from emigrating. The result was that many practised their religion in secret, while outwardly behaving like good Catholics. Others went even further and moved to the most isolated and remote part of the country, which was then, as now, Trás-os-Montes. Bragança thus became one of the most important centres of crypto-Judaism in the country. Over the centuries their rituals suffered and became almost secularised but they managed to survive. The regional cooking reflects Jewish influence, notably in the *alheira*, a sausage looking as if it was made with pork but in fact made without.

The area immediately to the north of Bragança, as far as the border with Spain, has been designated the **Montezinho Nature Park**. Though just as beautiful, it is much less well known than the park of Gerês in the Minho and as a result is emptier and less exploited. Leave town past the railway station, then turn right at the road marked for França, Portelho and Espanha. This road (N103–7) runs parallel with the River Sabor and takes you past a campsite, where there is a large wooden map, giving you details of roads and tracks. Many of these are unsurfaced but the route we took is easily manageable for all but the frailest of cars. Once again this is sparsely populated landscape, cultivated in the Sabor valley with vines and olives, but much of its broad and sweeping hills covered in low shrubs. *Lameira* is the name given locally to this terrain; pasture land which, when the grass grows high and the rains come, becomes very muddy.

In the old days, many cattle were brought up here for summer grazing, the herdsmen living 'wild' before returning from the mountains in the winter. Today livestock is less common but the villages are still amazingly self-contained and, in some cases, the land is owned and cultivated on a communal basis. People rarely marry outside the area and there is a proportion of blue-eyed blonds and red-heads startling even in an area where many trace their ancestry back to the Celts.

At **FRANÇA** there is a little church with a twin-belled tower typical of the area; there's also a centre for horse-riding. From here you start to climb, past the occasional cluster of beehives, towards the village of **MONTEZINHO** itself, which is straight ahead at the junction which marks Chã de Cruz to your right. After visiting the village, return and take the Chã de Cruz turning and at the next junction turn left for Soutelo. You are unlikely to meet any people, apart from the odd hunter, up here where it is rocky and bare. What you will see are birds: eight common partridge scuttled down the road in front of us and we also passed a grey heron standing perfectly motionless, on a small island in a reservoir. You might also see wolves or wild boar but this is rather unlikely. Camping is not encouraged in the park but bungalows may be rented by writing to Serviço Nacional de Parques, Rua da Lapa 73, 1200 Lisbon (01 675 259).

Eventually you descend from the plateau of the Serra de Montezinho down into the village of Soutelo, after which the road is resurfaced. Turn right near the bus-stop and keep going along a road lined with oaks and poplars, cross the Rio Baçeiro and continue through the villages of Paramio and Mofreita before turning right at the sign for Fresulfe. All this time the Serra da Coroa in the west has loomed up in front of you; at the next main junction after crossing the Rio Tuela you turn right onto the N103 and from here it is just another 8km to Vinhais.

The town of **VINHAIS** spills along the Chaves–Bragança road, its *pelourinho* and *igreja matriz* standing within what remains of the castle walls. We stayed at the **Pensão Riveirinha** (073 72490) whose front rooms provide a good view down into the Vale de Ribeiro de Trutas (valley of the trout stream). Just outside the town, to the west, is the dilapidated eighteenth-century convent of São Francisco, which has two churches, the lower one next to the cloister for convent use, the upper church for the lay brothers. It ceased functioning as a convent in the 1920s and is now a hostel for children.

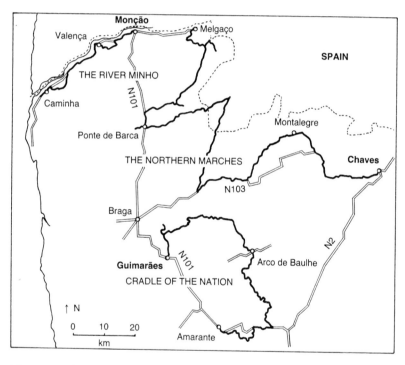

The region between the Minho and the Douro rivers includes the **Minho** and the **Douro Litoral**. It is bordered at the north by the Spanish province of Galicia with which it shares many cultural and linguistic characteristics. After the Moorish invasion of the peninsula in 710 AD the Minho area was abandoned, becoming a no man's land between the Christian kingdoms of the north and the Muslim territories. Today it is much more densely populated than neighbouring Trás-os-Montes but like that province it has a high level of emigration. The valleys of the three central rivers, the Cavado, the Lima and the Ave contribute to the region's fertility, making it the greenest in the country, able to yield two harvests each year. The Minho's inhabitants, Minhotos, are more religious and conservative than any other Portuguese and have the highest number of religious festivals and *romarias*. There are also many beautiful manor houses or *quintas*, few of which are ordinarily open to the public, although some of them offer accommodation as part of the Turismo de Habitação scheme. Many of these estates produce their own wine, particularly the sparkling *vinho verde*, best drunk fresh, close to its place of origin. Since half of the growers are small freeholders, you will often see, as you drive through the countryside, a novel method of training the vines upwards off the ground, even up the trunks and into the branches of trees, to avoid the damp.

The Northern Marches

3 days/240km/from Chaves to Melgaço

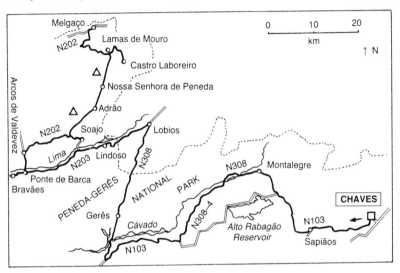

This route takes you from the windswept moorland around Montalegre (the Terras de Barroso), through the heavily forested Gerês park and along through the lush vegetation of the Lima valley. Until you reach the green heart of the Minho, the borderland with Spain seems sparsely populated and under-cultivated. As in Trás-os-Montes, many of the smaller villages organise themselves communally, with individuals working their own smallholdings but each household in turn pasturing the livestock. Many churches in the north of the province have small towers topped by an onion dome (not dissimilar to the shape of the haystacks).

CHAVES, which literally means 'keys', was founded by the Roman Emperor, Flavius Vespasian, as a halfway point between Braga and Astorga. The Romans called it Aquae Flaviae on account of its therapeutic hot springs. Its most notable remnant from this period is a fine arched bridge across the River Tamega with two inscribed milestones in its centre. Many of its houses are unusual for the profusion of ornate and brightly painted wooden balconies which either recede as the building gets higher or, more commonly, project to the extent that the upper floors almost touch each other from either side of the street. The Rua Direita has the best examples. The main square, the Praça de Camões, contains the remains of the castle, now a well-kept public garden with a military museum in the *torre de menagem*. Nearby is the unusual Misercórdia Church with a façade of twin barley-sugar columns below a statue of Nossa Senhora de Misericórdia. The interior contains floor-to-ceiling *azulejos* by Oliveira Bernardes, depicting (appropriately for a hospital church) miracles and acts of charity. Just below the castle walls is the large, modern **Pensão Jaime** (076 21273).

On the road west from Chaves (N103) you initially pass through agricultural land, the fields in late summer filled with haystacks, either shaped like the upper half of an onion or else thinner and more flame-like. The fields are interspersed with forests of pine and cedars, which start to dominate as you climb higher into the Serra do Larouço. Sixteen kilometres beyond Sapiãos, you take a turning right and climb another 13km northwards to reach **MONTALEGRE**. This is a small border stronghold of long standing, whose solid four-towered castle is perfectly situated on a high hill overlooking the River Cavado. Wellington stayed here on 18 May 1809, having decided to abandon the pursuit of the retreating French army, defeated at Oporto. There is one *pensão* here: the **Residencial Fidalgo** (076 52462).

From Montalegre, continue west along the N308. Follow the route of the River Cavado past a small dam, the Barragem de Alto Cavado, before crossing the river but still following it through Fiães do Rio and on southwards until you rejoin the N103 at another dam, the Barragem de Venda Nova. At this point, you pass from Trás-os-Montes to the Minho and the road winds and gradually begins to climb up through increasingly forested terrain. A series of blue signs indicate that you are approaching Gerês and, immediately after the sign for the **Pousada São Bento** (53 57190), you turn right, onto the N304, before crossing two successive bridges back across the Cavado. You are now in the National Park and from here the actual village of Gerês is only 8km away.

GERÊS, or Caldas do Gerês, is another famous spa, much visited even before the area was protected. You can take the waters between 1 May and 31 October. People queue at the colonnaded sanatorium for a pre-breakfast tin mug of water, handed to them by white-coated women. 'Aegri Surgent Sani' is written above the spring—'The sick will arise healthy'. You may also drink here a medicinal tea made from the Kneipp plant which, apparently, does wonders for the liver and kidneys. We stayed at the **Pensão Baltasar** (053 391 31) which was large and convivial and where you can also eat, but there are many other places to choose from, including some grand but rather faded nineteenth-century hotels on the main street.

The **Peneda-Gerês National Park** has been a protected area since 1971.

It consists of four mountain ranges at Peneda, Amarela, Soajo and Gerês (which is the highest). The forest area is mainly composed of oak, cork oak, yews, silver birch and holly, the cutting of which, at Christmas, proves hard to control. There are many plants and some animals unique to the area, like the *lirio do Gerês*, or Gerês iris, and the *garrano*, a small, shaggy brown pony of which there are about four herds. Deer, wildcat and possibly wolves also exist in the Park, though they are rarely seen, but the indigenous wild goat, a sub-species of the Pyrenean variety, is now, unfortunately, extinct.

The only drawback of the Park is that, despite its fame and popularity, it has still not been comprehensively mapped (or at least not recently), so that there are many discrepancies in the maps and guides issued to tourists, particularly when it comes to roads and footpaths. This is a shame, since Gerês is the perfect base for long walks (not a popular pastime with the Portuguese) but the information available from the two **Tourist Offices** (one in and one just north of the town) is limited. For the really intrepid, it is possible to rent cabins (*casas de abrigo*) by writing to the Parks Headquarters at Quinta das Parretas, Rodovia 4700 Braga.

From Caldas do Gerês you head north, still on the N308, towards Spain. After about 9.5 km, at Albergaria (very close to the border), the road to your left, marked for Campo de Gerês, is the site of the old Roman road from Braga, uniquely preserving a large number of its milestones. It follows the river, Rio do Homem and has great potential for excursions on foot. Otherwise, stay on the road north and soon, at Portela do Homem, you reach the border. According to some maps, there should be a road here, to your left, taking you to Lindoso. We found a track but it looked impassable by car, so rather than turn back, we decided to make a brief half-hour foray into Spain, unsurprisingly similar but for its greater cultivation. After passing through Lobios, you cross the River Limia (Lima in Portugal) and, at the main junction, you turn left at the sign for Aceredo and Portugal. We were in Spain for 27km but it was here, not in the Gerês Park, that we saw a small group of wild ponies grazing peacefully at the side of the road.

You re-enter Portugal just 5km from **LINDOSO**, another border fortification, whose imposing thirteenth-century castle can be seen from the road (N203). From here it is possible to follow the River Lima (which the Romans identified with the Lethe, the mythical river of forgetfulness) all the way to the sea, but on our route the next place to stop is the pretty and unspoiled town of **PONTE DE BARCA**. Despite being something of a traffic junction, this is a quiet and restful place. It used to be on the pilgrim route to Santiago de Compostela but, before the bridge was built, the pilgrims had to cross the river by boat, hence the name of the town. There is a well kept riverside garden, dedicated to the brothers Diogo Barnardes and Agostinho da Cruz, both poets of the sixteenth century. Next to the garden, overlooking the river, is a good restaurant, the **Bar do Rio**, where you can try the freshwater fish, particularly lampreys, for which the river is well known. It is also possible to hire boats and the river certainly looked clean enough to swim in. There are only a few places to stay in the town and the **Pensão Freitas** (058 42113) is probably the best of these. Some of the nearby *quintas* offer expensive accommodation: the **Paço de Gloria** (058 947177) at Jolda, about 10km west of the town on the other side of the river, is one such and the **Paço Vedro** (058 42117), just 2km away, another.

A short excursion, only 3km west of the town, takes you to **BRAVÃES** where there is a small and well-preserved Romanesque church, São Salvador. Its west and south portals are decorated with intricate carvings including monkeys and other grotesque figures, while the interior contains frescoes of São Sebastião and a Madonna and Child.

Leave Ponte de Barca by the ten-arched sixteenth-century bridge, which takes you north and onto the N101. After 4km, you approach the town of **ARCOS DE VALDEVEZ**. This is a prosperous market town about twice the size of Ponte de

Romanesque carving at Bravães

Barca and with some fine buildings, particularly those around the Terreiro do Centenarios at the top of the town overlooking the River Vez. The route, however, continues without entering the town, by following a turning to the right onto the N202 for Cabana Maior and Mezio. From here your ultimate destination is Melgaço but it is reached by travelling north-eastwards back into (the top section of) the National Park and through two mountain ranges via driveable, but sometimes unsurfaced, roads not marked on the Michelin map. The advantage of this route is some rugged but very beautiful scenery right in the heart of the Peneda range, but it should be avoided in wet weather.

But firstly, you continue along this road about 10km to Mezio, where you turn right for **SOAJO** just 4.5km further on. At Soajo (as at Lindoso) there is a particularly large concentration of *espigueiros*, odd-looking storehouses for grain and corn, common in the Minho, as well as in neighbouring Galicia. There are many local differences in their construction, though the ones around Soajo and Lindoso are almost exclusively made from granite and resemble miniature churches, or catafalques, placed on stilts. The pitched roofs are often surmounted at either end by crosses; the windows (for ventilation) are thin and shaped like lancets. Their most striking characteristic though, is the mushroom-shaped staddles supporting them, which prevent rats and mice from climbing up and eating the corn. The tendency to build *espigueiros* in groups isolated at the edge of town creates a slightly sinister effect when you first see them. At harvest, when the corn is stored, the stalks and leaves are not wasted but stacked to dry out for use as cattle fodder in winter. The stacks are tall and thin and are often attached at the top to the branches of a tree to prevent them from collapsing.

Fodder being carried to an espigueiro

Now our route begins its trip through the mountains by first heading back towards Mezio and then taking the right-hand turn for Adrão (about 1km short of Mezio). Soon the road becomes unsurfaced but manageable and you begin to climb through pine forests until you finally reach the mountain road and a dramatic panorama of the Peneda range. Pockets of cultivation are visible down below in the valley. The village of **NOSSA SENHORA DE PENEDA** is reached after a slow and gradual descent. Though extremely isolated, this is the site of an annual *romaria* and is completely dominated by its austere twin-towered church dedicated to Nossa Senhora da Peneda. Fourteen additional chapels, descending from steps facing the west end, testify to its popularity. Yet there is only one café here, the **Café Paris**, and no obvious visitor accommodation. From Peneda, the road is surfaced and straight, taking you through newly planted forest until you join the N202 just outside Lamas de Mouro.

There is a choice here between turning right for the village of Castro Laboreiro 8km away, or left for Melgaço. **CASTRO LABOREIRO** is an ancient settlement, supposedly with a ruined eleventh-century castle commanding fine views, which we completely failed to discover! What we did see was a rather old and mangy specimen of the interesting Castro

Laboreiro dog, an unusually large and sturdy breed with a thick coat of 'mustard and pepper' colouring, originally bred to protect the village from marauding wolves during hard winters.

Returning the way you came along the N202 will eventually take you, through milder, more cultivated country-side, to **MELGAÇO**. This is an old town but not very beautiful. Only 9km from the border, it has been occupied several times in its history, most famously by the forces of Juan of Castile, following his attempt to claim the Portuguese throne in 1385 (see p. 32). Legend has it that during the 52-day siege of the town, a woman disloyal to Portugal, known as *Arrenegada* (the Renegade), fought in single combat with another woman, Inês Negra, who had remained loyal. When their weapons broke, they fought hand to hand until Inês Negra was finally vic-

The village of Nossa Senhora de Peneda

torious. The following day, the siege was lifted when the Portuguese army, their spirits raised, scaled the walls of the town with the aid of a portable tower. The *torre de menagem* of the castle still stands, as do some of the outer walls. Below them, every Friday, sprawls a large, busy market selling everything from clothes to food and, when we visited, some cheap but good local pottery.

You can return to Ponte de Barca by taking the N202 to Monção and then the N101 south.

The River Minho

1–2 days/50km/from Monção to Caminha

As well as giving its name to the province, the River Minho acts as a natural north-western frontier between Portugal and Spain. Not surprisingly, freshwater fish (especially lampreys) are a local speciality. On this stretch of the river, the fishermen use tiny, oval-shaped boats called *batelas*, similar to the coracles once used by English fishermen, which are

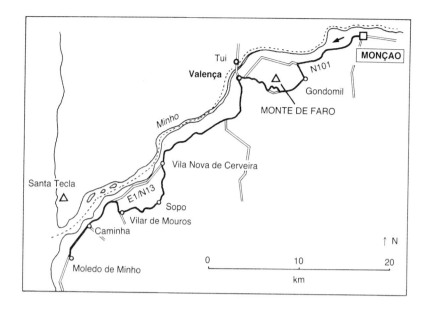

so light that they can be carried by one man on his back. The *vinho verde* from around Monção is particularly good with perhaps the best of all coming from the nearby Palaçio da Brejoeira.

The main square of **MONÇÃO** is named after, and contains a statue of, Deuladeu ('God has given') Martins, a local heroine, who helped to liberate the town in 1368. Besieged with her fellow citizens in the castle (which still stands) by the army of Henry II of Castile, Deuladeu baked some loaves with the last of the flour and had them thrown from the walls to the enemy. Demoralised to discover how well stocked the castle apparently was, the Castilians abandoned the siege. The grateful town commemorates this deed in its coat of arms, and in the bread rolls, *pãezinhos de Deuladeu*, which you can buy here. Just over 300 years later, her descendants erected a tomb for her in the *igreja matriz*. The church also contains an ornate Manueline chapel and a Romanesque portal. Monção faces the Spanish town of Salvatierra de Minho and the only surviving gate of the seventeenth-century fortress is named after it, the Porta de Salveterra.

We stayed in the large **Pensão Central** (051 52314) in the main square, which is cheap but not wholeheartedly recommended. The **Pensão Mané** has a better reputation and a good restaurant. Monção is another good place to try some of the locally produced *vinho verde*.

After leaving the town, head west along the N101, following the course of the river and passing on your right the medieval tower of **Lapela**, a border lookout post. The road continues to the ruined monastery of **São Fins de Friestas** but ignore the turning for Friestas and, instead, turn left at the sign for Gondomil. This takes you through forest before reaching the village at which point you turn right, passing the right side of the church, then on again through more forest. At the next junction turn right, following the sign for São Fins, and stop when the road becomes unsurfaced. From here the monastery is just five minutes walk across the valley. This is a beautifully situated and well-preserved Benedictine monastery whose building dates from the early twelfth century, although it was founded many centuries earlier. Dom Afonso Henriques endowed it with much of the surrounding land but its great wealth must have quickened its corruption, since by 1545 only three, dissolute, monks remained. There is a strange claustrophobic absence of sanctity to the place, even today, despite the beauty of its Romanesque church, which, like the one at Bravães, possesses fine animal and grotesque carvings above its doors and on its capitals.

From the monastery turn right and head for **Monte de Faro**, the highest point in the immediate area at 565m. At its summit, which provides marvellous views of the Minho, Spain and nearby Valença, there is a church, a good restaurant and a place to stay, the **Pensão Monte de Faro** (051 22411).

Descending from Monte de Faro, **VALENÇA** is just 6km away. This ancient fortress town was formerly called Contrasta as it is juxtaposed to the Spanish town of Tui just across the river, now easily reached by railway. The town is dominated by its perfectly preserved Vaubanesque fortifications, which on its inner walls alone, has no fewer than twelve angled bastions, which date from the struggles against Spain following the restoration of the Portuguese monarchy in 1640. Today the Spanish are rather more welcome and, indeed, swarm here, particularly at weekends, to spend their money at the numerous tourist shops along the narrow streets. The **Pousada de São Teotónio** (051 22242/52) is named after the Abbot of the Holy Cross monastery at Coimbra who became Portugal's first saint.

The road out of Valença, the N13, is practically a motorway and takes you through flat, open, rather dull countryside and by-passes the small town of **VILA NOVA DE CERVEIRA**. In fact, Vila Nova is another possible place to stay since the remains of its medieval castle now contain a luxury *pousada*. What we recommend, though, is continuing along the N13 a short while before turning left at the sign for Gondarém. This immediately takes you into hillier, partially wooded countryside and, after passing the lovely Solar of Casa Solarenga de Vireira (with two figures supporting family crests), you reach the **Estalagem da Boega** (51 95321). Named after one of the small islands near the mouth of the river, which are visible from here, this is a wonderfully civilised and extremely hospitable place to stay.

Continue west, passing an eighteenth-century Pieta in the village of **SOPO** before reaching **VILAR DE MOUROS**. Here, turn left before entering the town, cross a small medieval bridge over the River Coura, then, after passing a church, stay on this road which will take you all the way to Caminha.

CAMINHA lies at the mouth of the Minho and used to serve as a defence against the Spanish town of La Guardia (obscured by the mountain of Santa Tecla) but it is now a tranquil fishing port and no longer of strategic importance. It is practically surrounded by water since the River Coura, a tributary of the Minho, also has its mouth here. It was protected by attack from the sea by a fortress set on an island, the Insua de Santa Isidro, in the middle of the River Minho's estuary and by the Middle Ages had become a trading port of great prosperity. This is reflected in the splendid main square, the Praça do Conselheiro Silva Torres, bordered by the Town Hall, the clock-tower and merchants' houses on the south side. Finer still is the *igreja matriz*, one of the most beautiful and unspoilt churches in the whole of the north. It was begun in 1480 and contains both late Gothic and Renaissance elements. The intricate *artesonado*, or carved wood ceiling, is particularly spectacular and there is an unusual chapel, the Mareantes, with a miniature galleon hanging from its ceiling, which was built to house treasures found washed up on the beach in 1539.

There are several good restaurants in the town, including the **Restaurante Remo** (058 921459) and the cheaper **Restaurante Caminhense**. We stayed at the **Pensão Galo de Ouro** (058 921160), just off the main square, which also has a restaurant.

For a better view of the sea, there are several sandy beaches, fringed by pinewoods just a little way along near the mouth of the river at **Moledo do Minho**.

The Cradle of the Nation

2 days/150km/from Guimarães to Amarante

The Douro Litoral is a province rich in historical associations despite being practically deserted during the Moorish occupation. Guimarães was Portugal's first capital and, nearby, the Cîtania de Briteiros is the most complete example of a Celtiberian Iron Age settlement. From here the route wends east through gently undulating hills before crossing the Tamega, a major tributary of the Douro, and entering the forested Serra do Alvão, an isolated rural area close to Vila Real. Amarante, north east of the Serra, remains one of the most picturesque towns in the province.

Between 1095 and 1097, Alfonso VI of León and Castile granted his son-in-law, Henry of Burgundy, the County of Portugal. Henry fixed his court at **GUIMARÃES** where his son, Afonso Henriques, was born. On Henry's death, his wife, Dona Teresa, acting as regent, consolidated the territory but eventually fell out with her young son. In 1120, following the defeat of Teresa's forces at the Battle of São Mamede near Guimarães, Afonso Henriques banished her and declared himself Portugal's first king.

Because of its involvement in these events, Guimarães is known as the 'cradle of the nation', and today still prides itself on having been the new country's first capital. It is no longer a particularly important town, despite

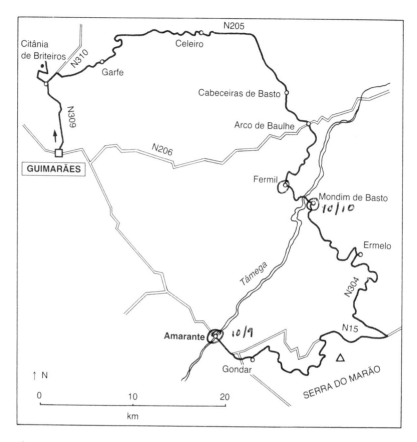

the increase of its textile and shoe-making industries, but it is a lively place, worth a day's visit for its historical associations and the fact that the old quarter is remarkably well preserved.

According to legend, Afonso Henriques was born and brought up in the great castle set above the town. Just below it, in the little Romanesque chapel of São Miguel, he was supposedly baptised. Continuing down the hill towards town takes you past the absurdly over-restored Paço dos Duques, once the home of the Dukes of Bragança, now a museum best avoided if you are short of time.

The attraction of the city is really the old town. Both the Rua da Rainha and the Rua da Santa Maria have some handsome houses, mainly seventeenth-century, with ornate wooden or iron balconies. These two streets meet at the Largo Senhora da Oliveira, named after the legend of the Visigoth Wamba, who agreed to be king only when his staff, which he had pushed into the ground, began to sprout olive leaves. Nearby is the **Museu Alberto Sampaio**, which has a good collection of ceramics. At the other end of the Rua da Rainha is the outstanding archaeological museum named after Martins Sarmento, who excavated the Citânia de Briteiros (see below). It contains much of interest, including a carved granite slab,

possibly a mausoleum front, known as the Pedra Formosa, and the so-
called Colossus of Pedralva, a large seated granite figure. Both were found
at Briteiros.

The **Hotel do Toural** (053 411 250), a good place to stay, is nearby, as
is the **Tourist Office**.

Leave the town and head north, not along the main road but past the
castle and then left onto the N309. After about 7km, you pass through the
village of Souto before crossing the N310 and after about 2km and a
gradual climb you reach the **Citânia de Briteiros**. This Iron Age hill
settlement—which is what a *citânia* is—probably dates from about 500BC,
when Celts from northern Europe first arrived in the peninsula. This one

The Citânia de Briteiros

survived into Roman times and may have been one of the last strongholds
against the Roman occupation. It was discovered in 1874, excavated the
following year by Martins Sarmento and is the most impressively complete
archaeological site in the country. The entrance is at the caretaker's
house, where you may buy a useful plan of the site. Set on a steeply sloping
hill, it contains the ruins of over 150, mostly circular, dwellings connected
be paved streets and protected by a series of ramparts. The two reconstructed dwellings are now thought to be inaccurate. Theories about the
precise function of all the buildings is constantly revised and argued over
by archaeologists and historians. It has recently been suggested that the
funerary chamber originally fronted by the Pedra Formosa may, in fact,
have been heated baths. The coins and artefacts originally found here are
now housed in the Museu Martins Sarmento in Guimarães.

Return to the junction and turn left onto the N310. This would take you to Póvoa de Lanhoso but instead, after a short while, take the first turning right to cross the River Ave and follow it eastwards through the village of Garfe. The road wiggles soon after passing Arosa, doubling back over the river and passing a series of small reservoirs before reaching Celeiro.

From here, the next stop is **CABECEIRAS DE BASTO**, the first of a series of towns and villages whose names are followed by the words 'de Basto', a reference to the pre-Roman inhabitants of this region, the Bastulos. This is another small place that has grown up around a great monastery, only the church now remains. The monastery was founded by Benedictines in the twelfth century but the twin-towered church, dedicated to São Miguel, dates from the eighteenth century. It contains an especially good example of the ornately carved organ-cases that are quite common in the Minho. This one has gilded satyrs supporting the pipes and several grotesque masks. In the square, not far from the church, is an ancient statue of a warrior, probably dating from Celtic times, although its moustachioed head was added very much later.

Continue south through the village of Arco de Baulhe (where the railway from Oporto terminates), past the village of Canedo de Basto before reaching Fermil, where you turn left. After 4km, you reach the River Tamega, a major tributary of the Douro which acts as a boundary with Trás-os-montes. On the other side is the small town of **MONDIM DE BASTO**. This is even smaller than Cabeceiras but, being right on the edge of the **Alvão National Park**, makes a good location from which to explore the rich and varied countryside. There is a **Tourist Office** on the main street, useful for maps and walking routes and also for finding places to stay if the **Pensão Mondinense** (38 23) is full up. The town contains some good eighteenth-century houses and a court house. Looming to its east is Monte Farinha, marked on the map by the name of the small church that surmounts it, Nossa Senhora da Graça. Its summit can be reached by car or on foot, which takes well over two hours, but is rewarded by an outstanding view.

Most of the area of the park, between the Alvão and the Marão mountains, is isolated and inaccessible, with several villages unreachable by car. The River Cabril, crossed by a Roman bridge, is just south of the town and can be followed upstream on foot. Otherwise, keep heading south along the N304 into increasingly wooded mountains. Shortly after crossing the River Olo, there is a turning left for **ERMELO**. We parked the car and walked there and found a small village essentially unchanged for hundreds of years. In fact, the granite lintel of one of the doorways had a date 1723 roughly carved into it. Most of the houses are made from pieces of schist packed together, with roofs of large loose slate tiles, and many follow the northern pattern of housing livestock on ground level and people on the upper floor. Since nearly all the houses are built on a hill, this means that the house may be entered, without stairs, from the uphill side. Despite a population of no more than 50, we saw two fishmongers in vans competing for trade when we visited.

Pressing on further, you reach the villages of Fervença and Varzigueto and finally the spectacular waterfall of **Fisgas de Ermelo**, caused by a band of quartz forming a step in the terrain between the higher levels of granite and the lower levels of schist.

Staying on the N304 and continuing south will take you to a major road, the N15, part of the planned motorway link from Oporto to Bragança. Turning left here would take you to Vila Real but we recommend turning right for **AMARANTE**, 35km to the west. On the left is the Marão mountain and 9km further on, the Pousada of São Gonçalo (55 461113).

Along with St John the Baptist (Oporto) and St. António (Lisbon), São Gonçalo is well known nationally as a *santo casamenteiro*, or matchmaking saint, and his legend is very much more important, not to say potent, than any historical reality. He came as a monk

A village house at Ermelo

from Guimarães in the thirteenth century, and is credited with restoring the prosperity of the town and even rebuilding the bridge across the Tamega. His ability to provide marriage partners, particularly husbands for old women, is a mystery but one to which many people devoutly subscribe. During São Gonçalo's *romaria*, the town's unmarried can offer each other phallic-shaped cakes as a declaration of intent, or they can tug at the girdle on the Saint's statue or touch his tomb. I assume that all these measures are equally effective. You can also buy (throughout the year) round, jellied sweets, which Gallop, in his book on Portugal, calls *testiculos de São Gonçalo*. These are extremely sweet.

The convent church dedicated to the saint is particularly beautiful. Begun in 1540, it is roofed over with red tiles and has a tiled cupola at its crossing. Its main entrance is through an ornate portico with statues of Saints Dominic and Francis. Inside, as well as São Gonçalo's tomb, there is another exotic organ case like the one at Cabeceiras de Basto. Unfortunately, the pipes have been removed. The cloisters have recently been converted into a museum of modern art, named after the town's most

Amarante

famous son, Amedeo de Sousa Cardoso, a painter closely associated with Cubism whose best work may be seen here. Facing the church and decorated with obelisks is the town's elegant eighteenth-century bridge.

There are several good restaurants overlooking the river: the **Zé de Calçada** (055 422023) is the most well known. The **Hotel Silva** (05 423 110) is a reasonable place to stay near the centre of town and in the same street as the **Tourist Office**.   *10/9/92*

7 THE BEIRAS

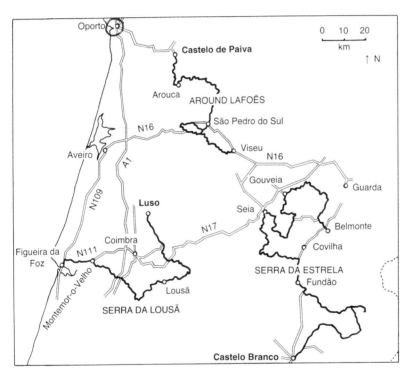

The middle region of Portugal between the Douro and the Tagus rivers is called the Beira, meaning edge or border. It is subdivided into three parts, **Beira Alta** (Upper), **Beira Baixa** (Lower) and **Beira Litoral** (Coastal). In its centre is the highest mountain range in the country, the Serra da Estrela, a bleak and dramatic landscape where resistance to the Roman invaders was led by the legendary Lusitanian warrior, Viriato. The mountains are continued to the south west by a smaller range, the Serra da Lousã, which gives way to milder, more fertile flatlands to the south of the Mondego river. Coimbra, the capital of the Beira Litoral and once of the whole country, stands on the Mondego. (Though not included on any of our routes, it may be considered worth a visit for the richness of its history and the beauty of its monuments.) Despite the fact that much of the region, particularly Beira Alta, is difficult to farm, it possesses two demarcated wine-producing areas: Bairrada, just to the north of Coimbra, and the larger and more famous Dão, named after the river that runs through it. The Dão wines are the most widely drunk table wines in Portugal, full-bodied, strong and a deep ruby colour, though they can sometimes be a little woody and harsh.

Around Lafões

2 days/125km/from Castelo de Paiva to Viseu

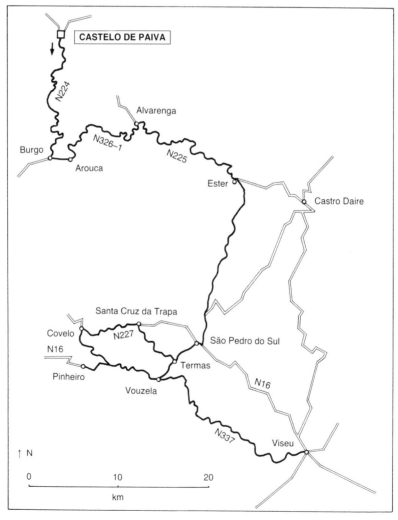

Lafões is the name of the old *concelho* (council) that used to administer this area. It no longer exists but the region is still referred to by the same name which derives from the Arabic word 'alafões' meaning two brothers, the brothers being the hills, Lafão and Castelo. Fed by several rivers, this is a fertile region which produces maize, vegetables, fruit and wine, but whose best-known product is veal (*vitela de Lafões*).

CASTELO DE PAIVA is close to Oporto and closer still to the river Douro. The town is mainly of interest as a starting point from which to explore the surrounding countryside. Our route begins by following in the direction of the river Paiva, south west along the winding N224. This takes you via the hills above the river, through forests of pine and eucalyptus. After about 22km turn left at Burgo and quite soon you reach the small town of **AROUCA**. There was a settlement here dating back to the Celts, which the Romans built up into a town, eventually destroyed by the Moors in 716. Today it is the vast, early eighteenth-century convent

that completely dominates the village. Founded in the tenth century, its fame and prosperity sprang from its connection with the country's first sainted Queen, Mafalda, daughter of Dom Sancho I. She entered the convent around 1220, having had her marriage to King Henry I of Castile annulled on the grounds of consanguinity. She persuaded the convent to adopt the Cistercian rule and led a life of piety. After her death her body is said to have shone with a great radiance.

The austerity of the convent's exterior with its heavily grilled windows belies the magnificence and subtle lighting to be found inside. The nave is flanked on either side by dramatic figures of female saints (mainly nuns) and the choir, which is screened off from the nave, contains ornately carved and gilded stalls incorporating paintings of the life of Saint Mafalda and other saints. The rest of the convent is now a museum of sacred art; guided tours take about an hour.

'*The death of Queen Mafalda*'

From Arouca, head eastwards along the N326–1 and shortly after crossing the Paiva you reach the village of **ALVARENGA**. There is just one shop here, which doubles as a bar and a restaurant serving good, simple food. The reason for stopping is to visit a series of twelve water-mills in the heart of a forest just outside the village. Follow the signs from the shop for the **Caminho dos Moinhos**. When you reach a cobbled path, continue on foot. A walk of about half an hour will take you to the mills, set on a steep hill down which tumbles a small but powerful stream. The mills are small, dry-stone sheds and only one now seems to be in working order, though an old man we met told us of the time when a constant procession of mules could be seen carrying grain to be milled for most of the surrounding villages.

From here make for **SÃO PEDRO DO SUL**, reached by heading south along the N255 which mainly follows the course of the Paiva as it twists its way through narrow gorges. Several almost completely inaccessible villages exist along the Paiva valley, their inhabitants venturing forth perhaps once or twice a year to purchase those provisions that they don't produce themselves.

After passing the villages of Cabril and Parada de Ester, leave the N225 at Ester and turn right, recrossing the Paiva before climbing once more into the hills. This passes through Sul before reaching a main road (N228) at São Felis. From here, **SÃO PEDRO DO SUL** is just 5km away, at the point where the river Sul meets the river Vouga. It's an attractive town with several fine buildings including the Baroque town hall which was once a convent.

Eight kilometres further east is the spa of **TERMAS**, which has been popular since Roman times. Portugal's first king, Dom Afonso Henriques, came here to recover after breaking his leg during an attempt to recapture Badajoz in 1168. The waters emerge at a temperature of 68.6°C and are believed to be particularly effective in the treatment of rheumatism and respiratory problems. There are several hotels, some quite new, as well as a good, riverside campsite at the nearby village of **SERRAZES**.

VOUZELA, some 3km south of Termas, is a small town in the heart of the Lafões area and considerably prettier than São Pedro do Sul. We stayed at the **Pensão Marqués** (77213), which possesses a charming family atmosphere. The owner's wife has won prizes for her *pasteis de Vouzela*, a light pastry cake known all over the country, while the home-brewed *bagaço*—a potent spirit made from the pips and skins left over from wine making—is worth a taste. There are several striking buildings in the town, notably the Misericórdia church with its blue-and-white tiled exterior and the thirteenth-century *igreja matriz* dedicated to a local saint, São Gil. The real beauty of Vouzela, though, lies in its location in the rich Vouga valley.

Leave the town, passing under the railway bridge and then turn towards Campia where, on the banks of the Alfusqueiro river, you can see (if you are there in late May or early June) the beautiful rhododendron that grows only here and in some parts of the Algarve. We then turned towards Oliveira de Frades and drove for 5km west along the main road to

PINHEIRO DE LAFÕES, where there is a remarkable buried dolmen, known as the Dolmen de Antelas, painted with geometrical and human figures in red and black and said to date from 4500BC.

From Oliveira de Frades you can take a longer route back to Vouzela via Covela and **SANTA CRUZ DA TRAPA**, where you can visit the ruins of the twelfth-century Cistercian monastery founded by Dom João Peculiar, Archbishop of Braga and Afonso Henriques' staunchest supporter. Only the church is still whole but in the gardens are the remains of an aqueduct that crossed over an old Roman road.

Continue eastwards to **VISEU**, the capital city of the Beira Alta. Its origins date back to an era even before the time the Romans used it as the main stop between Olissipo (Lisbon) and Bracara Augusta (Braga). The *Cava de Viriato* survives from those times: a Roman construction composed of a great octagonal wall probably built to protect a garrison, it may be seen on the left as you enter the town on the N16 from São Pedro do Sul.

The old part of the town lies to the right as you drive in. Its highest point is the Praça de Sé, a large handsome square, reached by steps, at the opposite ends of which stand the cathedral and the Baroque Misericórdia church. The cathedral retains much original Romanesque structure although the façade was rebuilt several times, the present version dating from the seventeenth century. The domed ceiling known as *abobada dos nos* is from the sixteenth century, its name derived from the ribbing: knotted cables carved in stone. The treasures of the cathedral are kept in the *sala do cabido*, and include the painted sculpture of the archangel Raphael with Tobias by Machado de Castro. The cathedral's Renaissance cloister is worth visiting too, but the interior of the magnificently-fronted Misericórdia church is very disappointing.

Rather more deserving of a visit is the adjacent *Museu de Grão-Vasco*, founded in 1915 and named after Vasco Fernandes, the great sixteenth-century painter who worked in this region and whose marvellous altarpiece from the cathedral forms the highlight of the collection. His famous depiction of St Peter, enthroned and wearing the papal cope and tiara, is here, as well as paintings by the Viseu school that developed around him. This image of St Peter is used as the label for one of the most well known Dão wines (Viseu stands at the northern end of the region), called, inevitably, Grão Vasco. There are many churches in Viseu but the main charm of this town is to be found in its narrow streets, where several mansion houses have ornately carved windows. The Rua Direita is the main thoroughfare, off which run several smaller streets where you can still find 'latoeiros', craftsmen who work with tin, at their work, as well as examples of the black pottery of nearby Mozelos. We recommend the **Cortiço** in Rua do Hilario as a good place to eat. Here you can try a Viseu speciality, *rancho*, a dish of chicken and beef stewed with various vegetables and served with a sprinkling of cumin—a real filler.

The town's most elegant hotel is the **Grão Vasco** in the Rua Gaspar Barreiros (032 235110) and there are two good *pensões* in Rua Alexandre Herculano, **Bela Vista** (26026) and **Dom Duarte** (25781) situated behind the **Tourist Office**, opposite the town's garden.

The Serra da Lousã

3 days/135km/from Luso to Figueira de Foz

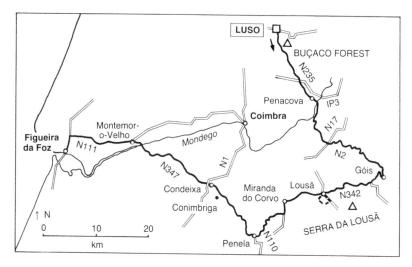

Fernando I of Castile and León was mainly responsible for pushing the border of the Christian territories south at the end of the eleventh century. Around Coimbra he created a new province in 1064, which was administered by the Mozarab Count Sesnando, a wealthy native landowner. This 'edge' (*beira*) of the reconquered lands was why the province is called the Beira. This route moves from the lush Forest of Buçaco down through the Serra da Lousã, a milder, south westerly continuation of the Serra da Estrela, and finally to the mouth of the Mondego river, which is crossed twice.

LUSO is yet another spa town, producing the most popular bottled water in the country. The success of the spa, from the middle of the nineteenth century, accounts for the disproportionately large amount of accommodation available. The **Pensão Portugal** (031 93158) offers particularly good value.

Luso is the logical stepping off point for a visit to the nearby **Forest of Buçaco**, a small but unique National Park, lying on the northern slopes of the Serra da Buçaco.

The forest was lived in and cared for by monks of various orders for over a thousand years, until 1834 when all the monasteries were dissolved and their property passed to the crown. Its greatest period of cultivation occurred after 1626 when the Archbishop of Braga presented it to the 'discalced', or barefoot, Carmelites. They enclosed the forest within a high wall, which still stands, and proceeded to plant a rich variety of trees, including the rare Mexican cedar, all of which were later protected by papal authorisation. Women were forbidden to enter the forest, which today is criss-crossed by a series of roads and footpaths and has ten gates within its walls (the Porta de Luso and the Porta das Ameias are the nearest to Luso).

There is much to see: the Avenida dos Cedros (an avenue of cedars, some extremely high) descends from the Porta de Coimbra to the Ermide de São José. Further south are the small chapels built for each station of the cross and culminating in the Cruz Alta (high cross) atop a hill. The Vale dos Fetos (valley of ferns) runs from the Porta das Lapas to the lake and nearby cascade. Of the monastery, little remains apart from the church, faced in black and white pebbles, and a few cork-lined cells. In its place stands the fantastic **Palace Hotel** (031 93101/2) built in 1907 as a summer palace for Dom Carlos just three years before the monarchy was overthrown. Stylistically, it crudely cobbles together almost every motif of Manueline architecture, from the Torre de Belém to Batalha, with predictably bizarre results. But it is undoubtedly luxurious and possesses one of the best-stocked wine-cellars in Portugal.

A hundred years earlier, in 1810, the Duke of Wellington came here, leading an army of about 30,000 men (half of whom were Portuguese) which succeeded in repulsing a larger French force before heading south to the fortified lines of Torres Vedras. To the south-east of the forest (through the Porta de Sula) there is a small military museum not far from the then unforested region where Wellington watched Massena's troops advance up to Mondego Valley. Each year a reconstruction of the battle is staged on site on the day it took place (27 September).

Continuing south along this road will eventually connect you with the main Luso–Penacova road, the N235. **PENACOVA** is an old town, marvellously situated high above the wooded banks of the Mondego river. Its main industry is the manufacture of tooth-picks (*palitos*) from willow wood. Descending from the town, you immediately cross the river and head south for 13km. When you reach the N17–E3, a major road, turn right onto it and after a few kilometres turn left, continuing south east along a winding road for Vila Nova do Ceira and **GÓIS**. The latter is a particularly beautiful spot lying in a sheltered valley through which the river Ceira runs. Its fine church contains the outstanding Renaissance tomb of Luis da Silveira and the bridge over the river dates from the sixteenth century. After crossing it, the road bends to the right; after 5km turn right for Lousã.

LOUSÃ is a smart, rather soulless town lying at the foot of the mountain range to which it gives its name and which is rather more interesting. There are several barely accessible and, in some cases, almost abandoned villages in the Serra da Lousã just a short distance from the town. These are worth seeking out either by car or, preferably, on foot (since the roads are unsurfaced) but you should first obtain a more detailed map from the Tourist Office and Museum at the **Câmara Municipal** in the centre of town. There are two ways of reaching the villages; in either case it is very easy to miss the turnings. What we did was to head south along a minor road following the railway line towards Vale de Maçeira. Just a short way out of town, after crossing a little bridge, there is a turning to your left which takes you into the woods. The tracks here are manageable by car; otherwise you could walk. There are several turnings which make the more detailed map essential. If all goes well, you pass by the practically abandoned villages of **CASAL NOVO, TALAS-VAL, VAQUEIRINHO** and **CATARREDOR**, after which you almost immediately regain the surfaced road, turning left to return to Lousã. All the villages are protected and recently EC money has begun to contribute to their restoration.

The other, less complicated , excursion is to the **castle of Lousã**, one of the most beautifully located of all Portugal's castles. It is supposedly the site of a vast hoard of treasure belonging to a certain King Arunce (he gives his name to the River Arouce) who fled here from Conimbriga with his daughter,

A village in Serra da Lousã

Peralta. What remains today is largely eleventh-century, refortified by Count Sesnando, a Mozarab given the task of revitalising the area following its recapture from the Moors. Nearby is the Sanctuary of Nossa Senhora da Piedade, close to a good alpine-style restaurant and an open-air swimming pool fed by a stream. There are several places to stay in Lousã and there is a campsite on the edge of town.

Twenty kilometres south west of Lousã is another, once important castle, **Penela**, where Count Sesnando was Alcaide. It continued for several centuries to be an important link in the line defending Coimbra. You reach it by heading west out of Lousã, skirting the Serra until you reach Miranda do Corvo, where you turn south along the N17–1 before turning right after about 2km for the short cut into the town. It is perched high on a hill with much of the rocky outcrop incorporated into the castle walls. The great earthquake of 1755 reached even this far north and much of the castle was destroyed but the view is still impressive.

From Penela, continue north along the main road (N374) until, approaching the village of Condeixa-a-Velha, you see a sign indicating **Conimbriga** to your left. Although the site was occupied by the Conii tribe many centuries before, it is as a late Roman settlement that it is most famous. The sturdiness of its hastily-built main wall, much of it containing fragments of old buildings, testifies to Conimbriga's vulnerability to barbarian attackers and between 465 and 468 AD it was duly besieged and captured by the Suevi. The surviving inhabitants gradually drifted to the greater safety of Coimbra (then called Aeminium). Excavations began in 1912 and although not much has survived above ground level, this is the most complete Roman archaeological site in the country. A villa just outside the later walls, between the settlement's two main entrances, contains some fine mosaic paving, partially reconstructed, with jets of water playing by an ornamental pool. Inside the walls there is a cistern once fed by the aqueduct that still runs parallel, with the main approach road and the remains of another villa with the public baths (thermae) nearby. Excavation is still going on and recently a museum has opened displaying many of the most significant finds. The entry charge covers both the site and the museum, which also contains a restaurant.

Mosaic floor at Conimbriga Roman villa

CONDEIXA-A-NOVA, a small town a few kilometres to the north, contains some good-looking seventeenth-century houses, notably the Casa Sotto Maior, as well as several places to eat. It is near the junction with the main road to Coimbra, but continue to head north west along the N347: from here the road follows the course of the river Ega, a tributary of the Mondego, and the surrounding countryside is highly fertile but increasingly flat.

As you approach the river Mondego, just after twice crossing the railway line, you see rising on the far side of it the impressive castle at

Montemor-o-Velho. This is quite close to the mouth of the river, which regularly floods the adjacent rice fields, sometimes as far inland as Coimbra. The castle was of great strategic significance and changed hands between Christian and Muslim several times. Ramiro I of León captured it in 848AD and entrusted it to an Abbot João about whom many legends have sprung up. One concerned the great rivalry between two knights, the Abbot's nephew, Bermudo, and a foundling named Garcia, whom the abbot had cared for. Feeling himself slighted, Garcia put himself at the disposal of the Caliph of Córdoba and attempted to recapture the castle for the Moors. Rather than surrender, the Abbot ordained that all the women and children within his care should be beheaded, while the men would fight on to the death. Their resistance was successful, Garcia was killed, and by a miracle all those beheaded came back to life but with a red line around their necks which supposedly was transmitted from generation to generation though we didn't notice it.

In 990AD, the great Muslim warrior, Al Mansur, devastated the region and it was not until 1034 that Fernando 'the Great' of Castile finally secured the castle, entrusting its control once again to Count Sesnando. The fortress church, dedicated to the Virgin, was built by Sesnando but almost entirely rebuilt in the sixteenth century and is essentially Manueline with spiralling columns in the nave.

The town is below the castle walls and its quietness belies its former importance, though there are several notable churches. In Nossa Senhora dos Anjos, a fifteenth-century church with a later façade, lies buried a local hero, Diogo de Azambuja, a soldier and adventurer who colonised the territory of São Jorge de Mina in the late fifteenth century. He founded the monastery to which this church belongs and his fine tomb shows him recumbent, armed and with a child at his feet.

There is nowhere to stay at Montemor, so continue west 15km along the Mondego until you reach the sea at **FIGUEIRA DE FOZ**, an important fishing port and resort popular with the Portuguese. It is not a very interesting town, however, although it has a good new museum, the **Museu Municipal do Dr Santos Rocha**, which contains a rich archaeological collection. Like many northern towns, Figueira de Foz celebrates the Feast of St John, 25 June—also the old solstice festival. People dance throughout the short midsummer night before plunging themselves into the sea for a 'holy' bathe. Among the many places to stay, we recommend the **Estalagem da Piscina** (033 22420).

The Serra da Estrela

4–5 days/430km/from Castelo Branco to Belmonte

This is the highest and most ruggedly beautiful part of the country. It is also the only place you can find snow, though not really enough to make good skiing feasible. In the summer it is still cool, and quiet; the Portuguese come here in the winter. The roads are winding but well

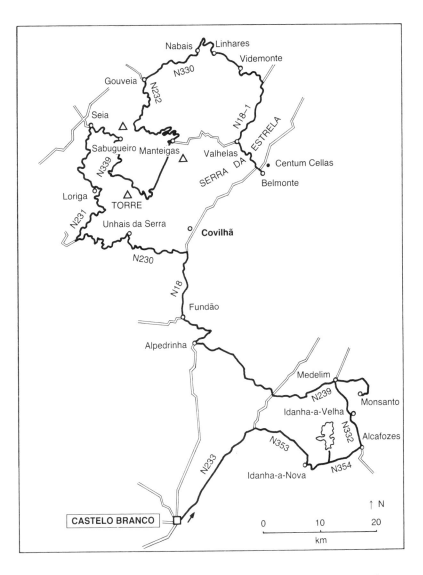

maintained and *miradouros* have been built where you can stop to admire the dramatic landscape. The descent from Manteigas to Belmonte is less wild, the granite crags giving way to forests and greater areas of cultivation.

CASTELO BRANCO (pop: 25,000) is the capital of Beira Beixa. The view from the top of the town stretches all the way to Nisa in the south and to Monsanto in the north. Looking down over the old town, one is struck by the harshness of the stone of the thirteenth-century cathedral which was enlarged in 1771 when the diocese of Guarda was split in two;

Castelo Branco was promoted to *cidade* (city) and made head of the new diocese.

It was the second bishop of the town, Vincent Ferrer, who improved the episcopal palace, where the **Museu de Francisco Tavares Proença Júnior** is now housed. The museum displays, among other things, local archaeological finds and some items of ethnographic interest. It also houses the workshop of the embroidery school where the famous Castelo Branco embroidered bedspreads are produced. The palace is best known for its eighteenth-century gardens with their rich display of Baroque statuary, which includes animals, evangelists and a series of the kings of Portugal (the Spanish rulers are somewhat shrunken). The statues are aligned along stone steps, trimmed hedges, water fountains and ponds, all of which make it a delight to visit on a hot summer's day (it's open from 9.00am to sunset). There are not many places to stay in Castelo Branco: we recommend the **Pensão Caravela** (072 23939) and there is also a campsite.

As you leave the town along the N233 for Penamacor, the landscape seems strikingly similar to that of the Alto Alentejo. Dry-stone walls divide the fields of pastureland, which are dotted with olive trees and smooth granite outcrops. 8km after Escalos de Cima, turn right for **IDANHA-A-NOVA** with the distant village of Monsanto visible on your left, perched on a hill. Idanha-a-Nova still has many traditional Beira two-storey houses, some of bare stone, others rendered and brightly painted with wooden balconies.

Continue east along the N354 until you see the sign for the Barragem da Idanha just 2km away. The reservoir was built in 1935 as part of an irrigation scheme to improve agriculture in this forgotten corner of the country. There is a simple restaurant here called **Adufe** and a campsite down by the water's edge.

Return to the N354 and follow it until the junction at Alcafozes. Here, turn left towards **IDANHA-A-VELHA**, which sits just below the Monsanto hill. The village is thought to occupy the site of a Roman town, called Egitania by the Visigoths, who built their cathedral above the Roman temple. The keeper and guide to the cathedral, personally involved in the first excavations of 1941, still remembers the area being used as a cemetery. The diggings uncovered the Visigothic floor some 1.5m below ground level, as well as the largest collection of Roman epigraphs ever found in a single spot. You can also see an inscription dating from 16BC—the oldest in the country. Just outside the cathedral is an old Visigothic font, a bishop's throne and a tank where *conversos* (Jews forced to profess Christianity) were immersed before being allowed to enter the church—this region was another centre of crypto-Judaism (see p. 82).

Travel north along the N332 before turning right for **MONSANTO**. This is a bizarrely primitive looking place with the houses and castle practically camouflaged by the great granite boulders which make up much of the terrain. The castle was badly damaged when its gunpowder magazine was struck by lightning in the early nineteenth century. Outside its wall are the ruins of the abandoned Romanesque chapel of São Miguel, once the village's parish church. Every year, on the feast of the Sacred

Cross (3 May), flowers are thrown from the castle wall to commemorate a legendary siege when the inhabitants placated (or disheartened) the enemy by throwing them a fattened calf.

Turn towards **ALPEDRINHA**, about 40km west of Monsanto along the N239. We stayed at the **Estalagem São Jorge** (075 57154) which has an excellent restaurant. There are several grand seventeenth- and eighteenth-century houses, including the Casa da Comenda and the ruined Paço do Picadeiro. In the courtyard outside the *igreja matriz*, we saw the remains of the *madeiro*—a huge log that is burnt for eight consecutive days during the Christmas festivities and around which the town gathers on Christmas Eve to sing carols and to exchange *filhoses*, fritters traditionally eaten at this time. The log must not be used for any other purpose than to start the fire at the next year's celebrations.

The drive from Alpedrinha to Fundão is a winding descent into the large valley known as Covada Beira, a fruit-growing region with a profusion of peach, apple, pear and apricot trees. Lacking a river and deep in the lowlands, this is not the place to be on a hot summer's day. The Marquis de Pombal encouraged the town's textile industry by creating a royal factory which now houses the town hall opposite the pelourinho.

By taking the N18 to Covhilha and then turning left to Tortosendo and Unhais da Serra (N230), you begin the climb up to the highest mountain in Portugal. On this side, the *serra* is strikingly bare, the steep sides of what appears to be a dome-like shape are covered by little other than shrubs. This may well change, however, since we noticed that terraces were being cut into the slopes, probably in order to grow eucalyptus trees for the paper industry. Nineteen kilometres on from Unhais, turn right towards Seia on the N231. The road takes you past the pretty villages of Alvoco da Serra, Loriga and Valezim and into deep coniferous forests where mountain streams tumble down the slopes, sometimes into man-made pools perfect for swimming.

SEIA is a busy textile town, whose recent growth has resulted in the hurried construction of some ugly modern buildings. The effect of these is soon forgotten, however, as you drive up and look down and view the town from the steeply rising road that then takes you to the highest village in Portugal, **SABUGEIRO**. It is worth stopping to admire the clear waters of the River Alva.

Here, up above the treeline, you can see great granite formations shaped by the elements to look like animals or people. After passing several reservoirs, the road reaches **Torre**, at 1993m the highest point of the Serra. A 7m tower (*torre*) has been constructed, which enables you to attain the height of exactly 2,000m. Unfortunately, the place has become something of a tourist trap, with local curios available for purchase at well above normal prices. A ski-lift has been installed here but skiing, a new sport for Portugal, is extremely unlikely to develop because of the dearth of good slopes and a lack of snow!

On the way down from Torre, turn left onto the N338 (not open during the winter) which takes you along the glacier valley of the Zêzere river all the way down to Manteigas. In this part of the *serra* it is quite easy to imagine that you are in the Alps; only the stone huts with their thatched roofs and the small patches of cultivated rye remind you that you are in Portugal.

Just before reaching Manteigas, at the spa of **CALDAS DE MANTEIGAS**, there is a turning to the right, marked for **Poço de Inferno** (Well of Hell). After a 6km drive through a forest of chestnut trees, firs and mountains ash, you reach the Poço—a spectacular waterfall that freezes in winter. If you are staying in Monteigas, this makes a good half-day trip or evening drive. We stayed at the quiet **Pensão Estrela** (075 47288) next to the Santa Maria church and dined on kid, a local speciality, at the excellent downstairs restaurant.

Manteigas is believed to have been the last stronghold of the warrior tribes who lived in the Herminios (the *serra*'s old name) and, led by the legendary Viriato, resisted the Roman invaders.

The road from Manteigas to Gouvela (N232) winds its way up the mountain side, offering a good view of the town and of the valley of the Zêzere. The road takes you past a campsite on the right, while further up you pass the **Pousada of São Lourenço** (075 47150). Shortly after the **pousada**, a turning to the left travels up to the Penhas Douradas, a meteorology observation centre with superb views to the east and the south. On the descent to Gouveia, as you drive past the turning to Seia, look back and you will see a curious granite rock by the side of the road known locally as the Cabeça do Velho (the old man's head).

Should you be tempted to buy a Serra da Estrela dog, there is a certified kennel on your left as you drive into **GOUVEIA**. Beware, however: the friendly, long-coated puppy grows up to about the size of a St Bernard. Like the Castro Laboreiro dog these were originally cross-bred with wolves and used largely as sheepdogs.

The town itself is fairly small but it is worth stopping to look at the eighteenth-century tiles on the town walls and at the earlier Casa da Torre. Gouveia is also a good place to try some of the famous Serra da Estrela cheese, *queijo da serra*. This soft, creamy cheese, which is sold wrapped in a cotton cloth, is still made traditionally by a method that dates back several centuries, but try to avoid cheap imitations sold at the roadside.

From Gouveia, take the N330 to Nabais and you will see the village of **FOLGOSINHO** (possibly the birthplace of Viriato) and its castle on your right before reaching Figueiro da Serra, where you turn right for **LINHARES**—a welcoming village but not geared to tourism, with no hotels and only a few cafés. Its castle, with those of Celerico and Trancoso, used to form part of the second defensive line on the Beira. Its origins are unknown but the present remains date mainly from the time of Dom Dinis. There are several fifteenth-century houses and the *igreja matriz* and Misercórdia contain some early Portuguese paintings, some possibly the work of Grão Vasco.

Driving up through Linhares takes you to an area of modern villas, at which point the road seems to peter out into a dirt track. However, after about 300m more it becomes a surfaced road and soon reaches the village of Videmonte. Here the mountains take on an altogether softer aspect and the road follows the valley until it reaches the main N18–1, which takes you through Famalicão and Valhelas.

After Valhelas, turn left onto the N232 towards Belmonte. Before turning into the town, make a detour about 1km north for a look at the **Torre Centum Cellas**, a tower almost certainly built by the Romans in the second century AD, possibly as a watchtower or a prison.

BELMONTE is another small village with a large castle. Over its main entrance is the carved coat-of-arms (two goats) of the Cabral family (*cabra* means goat), whose family manor forms part of the castle. Their most famous member was Pedro Álvares Cabral, born here c1467, who led the expedition which 'discovered' Brazil in 1500. The family memorials are in a chapel in the medieval São Tiago church but the statue of Nossa Senhora da Esperança which Pedro took with him on his expeditions is now housed in the village's other church. Once a prosperous town, by the beginning of the twentieth century Belmonte was relatively isolated and unimportant. It was probably due to this isolation that, at this period, Samuel Schwarz, a Jewish mining engineer from Poland, was able to discover here a community of *marranos*, or crypto-Jews, long after they were all thought to have been 'lost' through assimilation. In fact, they had always been regarded as Jews by their neighbours and had managed to preserve their identity by marrying among themselves and by maintaining the memory, if not always the practice, of Jewish observance (see pp. 82) Now they are returning to true Judaism and plan to build a new synagogue in the town.

There are a few cheap *pensões* in Belmonte but, if you want something more luxurious, there is the **Hotel Belsol** (075 91345) just outside the town on the main N18. The road leads back to Fundão and Castelo Branco.

A BRIEF HISTORICAL CHRONOLOGY

Portus Cale was what the Romans called present day Oporto. The name came to include the immediate vicinity, then the county and eventually the country.

During the second millenium BC, Iberian tribes enter the peninsula either from North Africa or Southern Europe. In the south west, Tartessian traders have links with western Mediterranean cultures including the Phoenicians.

From 700BC   Celtic invaders settle in Portugal. In subsequent centuries they mingle with Iberians to become Celtiberians. Galicia and northern Portugal dominated by Castro culture: people and livestock living within fortified hill settlements.

200BC   Romans occupy the peninsula. Resistance to the Romans by the Lusitani, a tribe living between the Douro and the Tagus, finally ends after the death of their leader Viriatus in 139BC.

27BC   Pacification of the peninsula by the Emperor Augustus. Hispania Ulterior is divided into provinces, Gallaecia (the north-west), Beatica (the south) and Lusitania (Estremadura and south of the Douro river).

From 200   Christianity established in the peninsula.

From 409   Invasion by the 'barbarian' tribes from Germany, the Suevi, the Vandals and the Alans.

415   Visigoths enter on behalf of the Romans and eventually drive out the Vandals and the Alans.

585   Visigoths conquer and take over the Suevian kingdom fixing their capital at Toledo.

711   Following disputes over the Visigothic succession, a large Muslim force, known collectively as Moors but, in fact, mainly Berbers from north Africa, conquer and occupy most of the peninsula.

718   The idea of the Christian reconquest begins in Asturias with a victory over a small Moorish force at Covadonga. The Christian Kings of Asturias-León gradually recover territories in the north west, culminating in the recapture of Oporto in 868.

For over 250 years, Muslim Spain (al-Andalus) is controlled by a succession of Emirs centred in Córdoba. The higher official positions are dominated by an Arab aristocracy. Religious toleration exists and many Jews assume positions of power and responsibility.

1009   Collapse of the Cordoba Caliphate. Al-Andalus divided into *taifas* (small kingdoms).

1050   Fernando I of León and Castile begins to expand his empire.

1064   Coimbra captured by Fernando and placed under the control of Davidiz, a Mozarab.

1086   Success of Christian reconquest leads to invasion of Almoravids from North Africa.

1097   Alfonso VI of León and Castile entrusts the County of Portucale (named after the Roman port of Portus Cale, present Oporto) to his son-in-law, Count Henry of Burgundy.

1128   Afonso Henriques, Count Henry's son, defeats the forces of his mother, Teresa, at the battle of São Mamede near Guimarães.

1139   Following a victory against the Moors at Campo Ourique in the Alentejo, Afonso Henriques declares himself king.

1143   Treaty of Zamora establishes the new kingdom's independence from León and Castile.

1147   With the help of the Crusaders, Lisbon is captured from the Moors. Almoravid empire superseded by the Almohads ('Uniters'), a new, fanatical Muslim group from North Africa.

1170   Portugal recognised as a kingdom by Pope Alexander III.

1249   Under Afonso III, the Moors are driven out of the Algarve.

1256   Lisbon replaces Coimbra as the capital.

1279–1325   Dom Dinis ('the farmer') strengthens his country's position by developing agriculture, refortifying border towns and centralising the administrative system.

1383   In the absence of a legitimate male heir, João of Avis, the bastard son of Pedro I, is elected king.

1385   Battle of Aljubarrota. Victory for João over a Castilian army supporting his half-sister Beatriz's claim to the throne.

1386   Ties with England strengthened by the Treaty of Windsor and, in 1387, the marriage of João I to Philippa of Lancaster, the daughter of John of Gaunt.

1415   The capture of Ceuta in Morocco initiates Portuguese imperialism.

From 1418   Henry 'the Navigator', youngest son of Dom João I, sets up a school of navigation at Sagres which, in turn, instigates the 'Discoveries' and Portugal's 'golden age' as a centre of world trade. Colonisation of Madeira (1419), the Azores (1427) and the Cape Verde Islands (1457).

1482   Diogo Cão finds the mouth of the Congo river.

1487   Bartolomeu Dias sails around the southern tip of Africa.

1496   Those Jews not expelled from the country are forcibly converted to Christianity.

1498   Vasco da Gama reaches India by sea.

1500   Pedro Álvares Cabral reaches Brazil.

1521–22   Part of a fleet commanded by Magalhães (Magellan) successfully circumnavigates the globe.

1531   Inquisition introduced into Portugal.

1557   Trading post set up at Macão in China.

1572   Publication of *The Lusiads* by Camões.

1578   Military expedition of Dom Sebastião to North Africa ends in devastating defeat and his death at the battle of Alcácer-Kibir.

1580   King Philip II of Spain occupies the country and claims the throne following the death of the cardinal King, Dom Henrique II.

1581–1640   Portugal now part of Spain and ruled by the Hapsburgs.

1607–1630   Loss of several important colonies, including the Moluccas and Ceylon, to the Dutch.

1640   The Restoration. In Lisbon a successful uprising against the Spanish is led by the Duke of Bragança, who becomes Dom João IV.

1661   Treaty of friendship with Britain and the marriage of Catherine of Bragança to the English king, Charles II.

1703   Methuen Treaty with Britain secures a market for English textiles in Portugal and a market for Portuguese wines in Britain.

1750–1757   The reign of Dom José I. The country is effectively governed by his reforming chief minister, the Marquis of Pombal.

1755   Earthquake devastates Lisbon, much of the Alentejan coast and the Algarve.

1759   Pombal expels the Jesuits.

1777   Accession of Dona Maria I ('the Mad'), a religious fanatic who reverses most of Pombal's reforms.

1801   Spanish/French alliance defeats Portugal, forcing the closure of Portuguese ports to British shipping.

1807   French army under General Junot invades Portugal for failing to comply with an ultimatum to declare war on Britain.

1808   French defeated by Wellington but allowed to withdraw under the terms of the Treaty of Sintra.

1811–20   While the Royal Family is in exile in Brazil, Portugal is governed, as a British protectorate, by Marshal Beresford.

1820–21   Liberal revolution intiated by army officers in Oporto. Liberal constitution accepted by the Prince Regent (later Dom João VI) on his return from Brazil.

1822   Independence of Brazil declared by Crown Prince Pedro.

1826   Pedro I of Brazil, now Pedro IV of Portugal, abdicates the Portuguese crown in favour of his seven-year-old daughter Maria but names his younger brother Miguel as regent.

1828   Miguel declares himself king and revokes the constitution.

1832–33   The Miguelist War or the War of the Two Brothers. Miguel is defeated by Pedro IV with help from the British.

1833   Monasteries dissolved and church lands sold off.

1834–53   Reign of Maria II. The liberals become divided into conservative 'Chartists' and radical 'Septembrists'.

1851–57   Virtual dictatorship of the Duke of Saldanha.

1861–89   During the reign of the constitutional monarch, Dom Luis I, the country is governed alternately by the conservative 'Regenerators' and the liberal 'Historicals'.

1890   Plan to link the colonies of Angola and Mozambique is thwarted by a British ultimatum. This leads to an unsuccessful revolt by Republican soldiers in 1891.

1908   Dom Carlos I and his heir are assassinated in Lisbon.

1910   End of the monarchy following Republican revolution.

1916   Portugal officially enters the Great War on the side of the Allies.

1930   Finance minister, Salazar, founds the fascist National Union party.

1932   Salazar becomes Prime Minister and in 1933 the Estado Novo (New State) comes into being. The fascist dictatorship bans strikes, censors the press and suppresses all opposition through its brutal secret police, the PIDE.

1939–45   In the Second World War Portugal is initially neutral but later permits British and American bases in the Azores.

1949   Portugal is a founder-member of NATO.

1961   India annexes Goa, a Portuguese colony.

1962–74   Colonial Wars in Angola and Mozambique. Caetano succeeds Salazar when he retires in 1968.

1974   The Carnation Revolution. A bloodless coup on 25 April led by the Armed Forces Movement (MFA), a group of dissatisfied young army officers, overthrows Caetano.

1975   Remaining colonies given independence.

1986   Portugal joins the EEC.

The Carnation Revolution and After

On 25 April 1974, the longest-running dictatorship in Western Europe came to an end in an almost bloodless coup known as the Revolution of Carnations after the thousands of red carnations carried by its supporters. The coup was organised and carried out by the Movimento das Forças Armadas (MFA), a group of radical army officers opposed to the Caetano regime and to the indefensible and increasingly draining colonial wars in Africa. General Spinola, a former commander in Guineau-Bissau, became President and, while the strong influence of the MFA continued, he appointed a largely left-wing coalition as the first of a series of provisional governments.

From the start there was conflict between those in power over the way that the revolutionary programme of decolonisation, nationalisation and land reform should be carried out. 1975 saw the independence of the colonies of Angola, Mozambique, São Tomé and the Cape Verde Islands and the subsequent influx of half a million refugees from these countries. It also saw increasing instability at home due to continued tension between political factions. Rumours of a left-wing coup led to pre-emptive military action on 25 November by Colonel Eanes (later to become President). Effectively a counter-revolutionary measure, it succeeded in all but ending the power of the MFA.

The Socialist Constitution, introduced the following year, established Portugal as a Republican parliamentary democracy. The Socialist Party, under Mario Soares, became the dominant party for the next few years but their failure to control the economy, despite heavy austerity measures imposed by the IMF, led to a gradual drift to the right. The current Social Democratic administration led by Professor Cavaco Silva, in power since 1987, has now almost entirely rid itself of the last of the revolutionary legislation.

BIBLIOGRAPHY

Portugal has a rich literary tradition and many foreign writers have given accounts of their travels there. Unfortunately, very little is currently in print, so much of what is recommended can be found only in libraries or second-hand bookshops. In Lisbon the Livraria Bucholz can be recommended for books and records. For the really keen, Lusitania Books, PO Box 132, Oxford, is also a reliable source.

Literature

Ballad of Dog's Beach *José Cardoso Pires*, (Everyman). Political thriller set in the 1960s.

Baltasar and Blimunda, *José Saramago* (Picador). The building of the great Palace-Convent of Mafra is the background for an unlikely love story by Portugal's most highly-rated contemporary novelist.

The Lusiads, *Luis de Camões* (Penguin). Published in 1572, this great verse epic blurs myth and history in telling of Portugal's seafaring triumphs—the Penguin edition is a good prose translation.

The Maias, *Eça de Queiroz* (Everyman). A masterpiece set in Lisbon in the 1880s. Eça wrote several great novels—**The Sin of Father Amaro, Cousin Basilio, The Illustrious House of Ramires**—all worth reading, none in print.

Selected Poems, *Fernando Pessoa* (Penguin). Portugal's most famous modern poet wrote under several different 'heteronyms' (separate artistic personalities). Other translations (with parallel texts) are **Sixty Portuguese Poems** (University of Wales Press) and **The Surprise of Being** (Angel Classics).

Travels in My Homeland, *Almeida Garrett* (Peter Owen). Quirky mixture of travelogue and philosophical romance by Portugal's leading Romantic writer. First published in 1846.

The Wondrous Physician, *Jorge de Sena* (Everyman). Medieval fantasy by a twentieth-century poet. By the same author, **By the Rivers of Babylon** (Polygon) is a collection of fantastical short stories.

History

History of Portugal, *A.H. de Oliveira Marques* (Columbia University Press). Long, but by far the best general history in English.

Portugal: Fifty Years of Dictatorship, *António de Figueiredo* (Pelican). Good analysis of the Salazar years.

The Portuguese Seaborne Empire, *C.R. Boxer* (Pelican).

Prince Henry the Navigator, *John Ure* (Constable). Good introduction.

Revolution and Counter-Revolution in Portugal, *Martin Kayman* (Merlin). Extremely detailed account of 1974 and its aftermath.
Spain and Portugal: The Prehistory of the Iberian Peninsula, *H.N. Savory* (Thames and Hudson).
The Third Portuguese Empire 1825–1975, *Gervase Clarence-Smith* (Manchester University Press).

Art and Architecture
The Arts of Portugal 1500–1800, *Robert C. Smith* (Weidenfeld). Well illustrated 'classic' text.
Country Manors in Portugal, *Marcus Binney* (Antique Collectors Club).
The Finest Castles in Portugal, *Julio Gil* (Verbo). **Arquitectura Popular em Portugal** (Associação dos Arquitectos Portugueses). Three-volume survey of vernacular architecture in Portuguese but with many illustrations.
Portuguese Plain Architecture 1521–1706, *George Kubler* (Wesleyan University Press).

Travel
The Bible in Spain, *George Borrow* (Century). His eccentric attempt to distribute bibles in Portugal and Spain.
Blue Guide Portugal, *Ian Robertson* (A & C Black).
Journal of a Voyage to Lisbon, *Henry Fielding* (Everyman). Marvelously entertaining account of the horrors of travelling when ill.
Journal of William Beckford in Portugal and Spain, *Boyd Alexander* ed. (Rupert Hart-Davis).
Journals of a Residence in Portugal 1800–1801, *Robert Southey* (Oxford).
Lisbon: City as Art, *Brigid Brophy* from **Reads: A Collection of Essays** (Cardinal).
Portugal, A Book of Folk-Ways, *Rodney Gallop* (Cambridge). Indispensible survey of sacred and secular folk-lore.
Portuguese Reveries, *Hans Magnus Enzenberger* from **Europe, Europe** (Picador).
Recollections of an Excursion to the Monasteries of Alcobaça and Batalha, *William Beckford* (Centaur Press).
They Went to Portugal, *Rose Macaulay* (Penguin). Highly entertaining character sketches of English travellers. There is also a second volume, **They Went to Portugal Too** (Carcanet).

Food and Drink
Cozinha Tradicional Portuguesa, *Maria de Lourdes Modesto* (Verbo). Available in English but only in Portugal.
The Food of Portugal, *Jean Anderson* (Robert Hale).
The Wines of Portugal, *Jan Read* (Faber).

Language
Discovering Portugal (BBC) Two tapes and a book, very good introduction.
Just Enough Portuguese (Passport Books) Useful for emergencies.

INDEX

Index